Andrássy Studien zur Europaforschung

Volume 23

Volker Stanzel [ed.]

New Realities in Foreign Affairs

Diplomacy in the 21st Century

Nomos

The Deutsche Nationalbibliothek lists this publication in the Deutsche Nationalbibliografie; detailed bibliographic data are available on the Internet at http://dnb.d-nb.de

ISBN 978-3-8487-5776-3 (Print)
978-3-8452-9950-1 (ePDF)

British Library Cataloguing-in-Publication Data
A catalogue record for this book is available from the British Library.

ISBN 978-3-8487-5776-3 (Print)
978-3-8452-9950-1 (ePDF)

Library of Congress Cataloging-in-Publication Data
Stanzel, Volker
New Realities in Foreign Affairs
Diplomacy in the 21st Century
Volker Stanzel (ed.)
127 pp.
Includes bibliographic references.

ISBN 978-3-8487-5776-3 (Print)
978-3-8452-9950-1 (ePDF)

1st Edition 2019

Table of Contents

Abbreviations

AA	Association Agreement
AfD	Alternative for Germany
AI	artificial intelligence
AR	augmented reality
BDI	Federation of German Industries
BRICS	Brazil, Russia, India, China, South Africa
CCTV	Closed Circuit Television
CFSP	Common Foreign and Security Policy (EU)
CPG	Civil Protection Group (NATO)
CVE	counter violent extremism
DCFTA	Deep and Comprehensive Free Trade Area
DDS	digital diplomatic system
DEI	digital emotional intelligence
DNA	desoxyribonucleic acid
EADR-CC	Euro-Atlantic Disaster Response Coordination Centre
ECOSOC	Economic and Social Council (UN)
EEAS	European External Action Service
EIA	economic integration agreement
EP	Eastern Partnership
EU	European Union
FAC	Foreign Affairs Council
FPA	foreign policy autism
FTA	free trade agreement
G7/8	Group of Seven/Group of Eight
G20	Gruppe of Twenty
IARPA	Intelligence Advanced Research Projects Activity
IFIs	International Financial Institutions

IO	international organization
IR	International Relations
ISIS	Islamic State in Iraq and the Levant
IT	Information Technology
JHAFG	Joint Health Agriculture and Food Group
MFAs	Ministries of Foreign Affairs
MIKTA	Mexico, Indonesia, South Korea, Turkey, Australia
MR	mixed reality
MSF	Médecins sans frontières
NATO	North Atlantic Treaty Organization
NDS	National Diplomatic System
NGO	Non-Governmental Organization
OFAC	Office of Foreign Assets Control (U.S.)
Oxfam	Oxford Committee for Famine Relief
PTA	preferential trade agreement
TNA	transnational actor
TTIP	Transatlantic Trade and Investment Partnership
UN	United Nations
VR	virtual reality
WTO	World Trade Organization

Issues and Recommendations

Modern diplomacy extends its activities into many spheres, but today it is subject to unprecedented influences and restrictions. An example of its diversifying influence is reflected in the expansion of the framework and themes of traditional multilateral diplomacy: the UN Climate Change Conference in Bonn in 2017 was the largest multilateral conference ever held in Germany; issues such as climate and health, which in the past were by no means part of the foreign policy realm, are handled by diplomatic means today as a matter of course. At the same time, in some areas of international relations, policy makers are turning away from multilateralism – and it is not just U.S. President Donald Trump, who assumes that foreign policy issues are better solved bilaterally. Finally, the public, in turn, is more directly –often mediated by social media – placing demands on diplomacy, be it to stop whaling, halt the flow of refugees, or any other issue on the contemporary agenda.

Such change has become increasingly noticeable in the decades since the end of the Cold War, or perhaps it is an altogether recent emergence. The new expansions of and restrictions on diplomacy deserve academic consideration, if only because of its influence on the politics of modern states. During the years 2016 to 2018, a working group named *Diplomacy in the 21st Century* has taken on the task of more thoroughly and comprehensively examining today's diplomacy at the Stiftung Wissenschaft und Politik – German Institute for International and Security Affairs (SWP) in Berlin, financially supported by the German Federal Foreign Office and ZEIT-Stiftung.

Modern diplomacy is in the midst of a process of change, and that rate of change is likely to approximately match the pace of general change in modern industrial societies. However, diplomats' responses to modern challenges often fall under the radar of governments and the public, precisely because they do not conform to what is traditionally considered to be typically diplomatic. Nevertheless, at the same time they have a strong influence on the actions and self-understanding of governments, and probably also on the public's understanding of foreign policy.

Rapid changes in the character of modern diplomacy are well recognized by those who are accustomed to being active in diplomacy, to be affected by it or to observe it, and the fact that diplomats are trying to navigate the implications of rapid changes is demonstrated by several recent developments. A variety of reform efforts – in Germany, pursuant to the comprehensive 'Review' analysis undertaken in 2014 – endeavour to exchange information between the foreign ministries of the EU member states with regard to the need for reform and the reforms currently under way. The fact that even China is dealing with questions of modern diplomacy highlights the significance of the emerging changes in the nature of diplomacy.

Such shifts in the focus of diplomatic activity raise questions about which changes in modern diplomacy will have longer term impacts, as well as if and how governments should respond to those changes. Four aspects concerning diplomacy seem to be of central importance: (1) The personality of the individual diplomat; (2) fundamental changes that come with technical developments, especially due to digitization; (3) the increase of diplomatically active actors; (4) the new sensitivities of various publics to foreign policies.

The heterogeneity and pluralism of thinking about modern societies impacts the diplomat's personality and their work as much as anyone else. An example might be what occurs through the use of social media: even the way a diplomat uses social media constitutes a 'message' from the diplomat's society to the outside world beyond what a government wants to officially communicate. This changes the appearance and presumably the orientation of diplomacy and must be taken into account in the recruitment, training and employment of diplomats.

As a matter of course, governments are always using new technical *instruments*. The means of *digitization*, for example, thus intervene in the functioning of administrative action. Such intervention can hinder or accelerate diplomacy, for example in the collection and processing of information. Furthermore, digitization influenced by social media in turn influences the preservation, gain, and loss of trust in the public of a country and its international partners.

A number of *new actors* involve themselves in diplomatic processes on their own initiative and/or are deliberately involved in dealing with new tasks of diplomacy. These actors include other national institutions, such as other ministries whose tasks extend into foreign policy, to international organizations – mostly UN sub-organizations – or, for Europeans, to EU institutions. They may include transnational companies and non-governmental organizations. At the same time, when diplomats appear more visible to the public thanks to the digital revolution, they stand more in the shadow of other foreign policy actors. In fact, professional diplomacy as a whole tends to be overshadowed at least partially by the activities of traditionally non-diplomatic actors.

Lastly, and incessantly, new and often highly emotional sensitivities of *publics* arise, and these too make use of social media to communicate with one another. When making demands of governments, and when governments wish to accommodate those demands, the problem of the democratic legitimacy of such publics and their demands immediately arises.

All of these factors are becoming increasingly impactful as a result of the progress of inter-state exchange and domestic connectivity of state action, and possibly even the shifting moods of relevant individuals. These factors signify and reinforce the trend of traditional diplomacy's diminishing influence. This tendency, as it reflects overall societal developments, needs to be absorbed by diplomacy as a part of governance of a state. If well directed, changes in diplomacy may be able to inform future governments' actions and the societies that represent them. Therefore:

Diplomats must understand the tension between the condition of the individual and state requirements, and engage with that tension without detriment to the state.

Digitization must be used in such a way that gains in efficiency are not made at the expense of efficacy;

it is important to develop forms of mediation and reconciliation of the interests of both sides that allow governments to operate as sovereign states, but at the same time make use of the influence and the potential of other actors;

dealing with publics is likely to raise the gravest problems and requires the development of new and more open forms of state activity that respond to the ways in which emotionalized publics who wish to participate in governance express themselves.

At the same time, the principles of representative democracy must be kept intact; if not, the state will suffer damage to the legitimacy of its system of governance. The crucial question will be how governments can ensure sufficient efficacy and efficiency, and thus also their legitimacy, to be able to address adequately the needs of a state.

Introduction: Following the Wrong Track or Walking on Stepping Stones – Which Way for Diplomacy?

Volker Stanzel

Diplomacy, like so many areas of public administration, is affected by the radical changes of the 21st century. Shocks within the international order, the revolution of internet-based global communication, and legitimacy problems of liberal governments seem to necessitate a fundamental re-orientation of foreign policy tools. Otto von Bismarck, first chancellor of the German empire of 1871, described diplomacy as the never-ending negotiation of reciprocal concessions between states. If that is the case, then today we face the question of the purpose of such a time-consuming art of managing international relations.

In early 2016, the Working Group *Diplomacy in the 21st Century* was established at the Stiftung Wissenschaft und Politik – German Institute for International and Security Affairs (SWP), with the financial support of the German Foreign Ministry and the ZEIT-Stiftung. The group is composed of diplomats, observers, and researchers from Germany, Australia, Canada, China, Denmark, France, Great Britain, India, the Netherlands, Norway, Russia, Sweden, and the United States (U.S.). In contrast to the 2014 'Review'[1] of the German Foreign Ministry, which examined German foreign policy and the structures of the German Foreign Office, the research approach of the SWP is narrower. Its insights into modern diplomacy, however, concern not only Germany. The central question for the practitioners and researchers of the working group was whether global changes of the 21st century necessitate changes at the very core of diplomacy in order for it to function effectively and efficiently, as well as to preserve its legitimacy as a foreign policy tool of governmental action. The essays in this volume

1 After beginning his second term as Foreign Minister at the end of 2013, Frank-Walter Steinmeier initiated a year-long public debate among German and non-German experts and interested observers about the goals and instruments of Germany's foreign policy, concluding with the decision to make a number of major structural changes in the ministry. See Auswärtiges Amt, ed., *Review 2014. Crisis – Order – Europe*, Berlin 2014, https://www.auswaertiges-amt.de/blob/692042/cef1f6308ebdb0d2d7c62725089c4198/review2014-data.pdf (accessed 3 May 2018).

from participants of the working group reflect a broad spectrum of analyses. We arranged them according to (1) personal, (2) instrumental, (3) institutional as well as (4) global elements.

*

Beyond Bismarck's simple description of diplomacy, things become complicated. Therefore, the working group of the SWP restricted itself to a rough definition of diplomacy as the touchstone for its discussion (not necessarily incorporating every member's individual definition): a pragmatic approach to manage the relations between states and other institutions in the intergovernmental space with the aim of arriving at peaceful conflict resolutions. *Sascha Lohmann* approaches the problem of a definition in his chapter when he describes modern diplomacy employing economic instruments and turning markets into a new 'battlefield.' Changes in the structure of the international community have made continual adaptations in diplomacy tactics necessary. An example of change to diplomatic organization is the 15th century shift from temporarily posted legations by governments to the establishment of permanent residing ambassadors. Similarly far-reaching adaptations might be required again today, since there is not only a greater public interest in diplomatic activity, but also growing demand by publics to participate in matters that have traditionally been under the purview of diplomats and governing bodies. Additionally, new communication devices and a growing number of state and non-state actors influence foreign policy.

1. *The Personal Element*

Diplomats are bureaucrats of sorts, and certain traits of their personalities play significant roles in their specific professional activities. Negotiations in general possess an official character, but informal communication between persons through expressions of behaviour reflect the complexity of the negotiations, the need for confidentiality, and discretion ranging from formality to informality determines the degree of its effectiveness. Charm, persuasion, or restraint may seem like clichés; however, they constitute essential features of communicative behaviour and correlate more with a person's character than one's training. In today's secular and pluralistic societies, moral standards likewise depend more on a person's characteristics than on specific training. Due to immigration and globalization today, diverse cultures that were once bounded by oceans and continents interweave more than in the past; people of diverse backgrounds now find themselves in the same public spaces, and there are simply more stimuli to personally witness and reflect on, problems such as unequal treatment of people based on gender, age, race, or other ascribed characteristics. Increasing social diversity can make moral conflicts matters of conscience more readily than in the more homogenous societies of the past. Individual civil servants can feel obligated to resist their superiors' instructions – in the case of Germany in accordance with Article 20 of German Basic Law[2] – and become a whistleblower.

Today, this social diversification, and in some ways even fragmentation, reaches far. Language skills are more widespread, and to 'digital natives' the operation of new technologies comes naturally, while the functionaries of the past struggle to make sense of and use new communication pathways. The comprehension of gender equality and the values of private family life come from but also influence individuals' outlooks on and participation in society generally. And these are only a few examples. All in all, personal values constitute a diplomat's 'message', which informs the image of his country as well as the reactions of his host country. While the recruitment of future diplomats should follow precise criteria, one question remains on which *Christer Jönsson* elaborates in his chapter: to what degree can today's diplomats as individuals still satisfactorily represent their ever more heterogeneous societies?

In a society that asks how bureaucracies can fulfil their task of supporting political decisions meaningfully by rationally applying information and knowledge, there is some temptation for political leaders to stigmatize the traditional civil service as old-fashioned and inherently error-prone. *Andrew Cooper* analyses this question further in his chapter. At the same time, decisions made at the top of the hierarchy may be adapted to what they regard as the requirements of society by civil servants even at the lower operational level. Hierarchy and bureaucratization have always been the means to restrict accumulation of power. However, the high level of external influences besides the government or even outside of the state reduces the influence of individual diplomats. This imbalance might even threaten the democratic principle of the responsibility of governmental action.

---

2 Basic Law (i.e. Germany's constitution) Article 20 (4): "All Germans shall have the right to resist any person seeking to abolish this constitutional order, if no other remedy is available.".

2. *Instrumental Level: Digitization*

The improvements of modern communication technology have complex effects on diplomatic action. *Corneliu Bjola* points out in his chapter that digitization "is likely to penetrate the deep core of the diplomatic DNA." This can promote creativity, but also destroy existing structures of communication and its organization. *Emillie V. de Keulenaar* and *Jan Melissen* argue that existing 'analogue' diplomacy is not merely superimposed onto technologies now shaping an environment that is facilitating digitally native practices. Their analysis gives recommendations for diplomatic practitioners who still look at new technologies, including social media, as merely open and freely available 'services.' Amongst all the 'instruments' of diplomacy we will focus specifically on digitization by looking at three key factors: unprecedented time restraints for decision-making; the necessity to distil a high volume of incoming information responsibly; and the integration of social media.

(1) The timeframe to respond to an incident is continually shortened due to the increasingly rapid transmission of information between embassies abroad and foreign ministries, as well as between other foreign policy actors. Consequently, this rapidity places an increasing burden on the persons acting at the top of a hierarchy and in positions where proposals for decisions are worked out. This burden can be quantified as the period of time available for the receipt of an item of information and subsequent consultation about it: the less time there is, the greater the pressure on the decision maker. Due to accelerating information transmission, only a limited range of issues reach the level of the responsible decision makers. Therefore, tensions arise between the expectation for quick action on the basis of comprehensive information on the one hand, and the necessity to act conscientiously on the basis of deliberated information on the other. Physical factors such as lengthy nightly conferences, travel across multiple time zones, and overloaded schedules only add to the strain. Despite the rising number of people responsible for the distillation of information and tactics for reducing the information to be taken into account, no solution has been found to reduce pressure on the decision-making process. Therefore there is a greater risk that wrong decisions will be made, not due to an erroneous comprehension of the known facts (a risk always at hand given the imperfection and incompleteness of human knowledge), but because time is restricted for the processing of and reflection on facts and possible courses of action.

(2) Information frequently travels on non-diplomatic paths, such as in social media. This gives opportunities to actors such as large corporations

or civil society organizations competing with governments in some areas to act independently of and possibly earlier than a government. Therefore, instead of only gathering information, diplomacy must also distil it usefully and competently. Among other things, diplomacy involves the "provision of knowledge."[3] However, today, diplomacy has to be more the distillation of knowledge – and in real time. Transcending mere knowledge distillation is the only way to process information into reasonably argued proposals for actions for political decision makers. The danger is that decision-making is integrated into the technological procedures without undergoing a thorough examination to see if the information can be made available quickly and avoid being superficial – which is essential. Modern digital diplomatic communication strives to make it possible to react to events in real-time. However, digital communication has to balance efficiency enhancement through increased speed, and effectiveness enhancement through calculability. This balance, if successfully reached, enhances trust on the side of the 'consumer' of foreign policy. Hence, the 'cultivation of trust' is also a fitting description of modern diplomatic activity.

(3) Currently, governmental action is under constant scrutiny by the public. Social media did not trigger this scrutiny, but they transport it and the pursuant conversations. Thus, social media are themselves instruments of diplomatic action. These actions are not, as in the past, soliloquized 'public relations work.' However, they strive to promote dialogue with domestic and international publics. Therefore, modern diplomats are unavoidably under pressure to use social media. This means that they are approachable and open to public criticism via digital platforms. Social media exchange with official dialogue partners and interested publics creates a far-reaching network of connections with known and unknown, influential and powerless actors, observers, and participants. Simultaneously this exchange has to adapt to the linguistic and formal character of the new media. Independent of their actual added value for the workings of diplomacy, social media impact on all those actors in a general manner – when for example malice is directed toward a politician – as well as in specific cases – when their users, for example, ask about certain foreign policy activities. Due to their influence on publics, which can be expedited by commercialized or in other ways motivated sensationalism, distorted reporting or fake news (therefore not much different from that of the traditional me-

3 See Iver B. Neumann, *At Home with the Diplomats: Inside a European Foreign Ministry* (Ithaca, NY, and London: Cornell University Press, 2012), 7.

dia), social media even have the strength to create pseudo-crises, some of which may waste substantial resources.

A deeper risk of the use of social media by diplomats is that it might reorient itself toward the public's opinions about foreign policy matters. Currently, politics must be presentable and comprehensible for many publics. The need to communicate quickly and effectively with diverse publics results in oversimplified explanations that fail to reflect the true complexities of the matters at hand. That oversimplification to the detriment of complexity in turn risks affecting actual politics: decisions may be made only so that they are more easily comprehensible – leading to difficult ethical questions. Crisis management is probably most susceptible to this risk because it is where measures of foreign policy concern the lives of individuals most directly. Yet the impacts of social media are strongest on the formulation and conception of diplomacy and foreign policy, where the danger for the publics' trust in decision-makers is greatest.

3. *Institutional Aspects*

Essentially, diplomacy operates in the framework of a community within completely sovereign nation states. Nevertheless, with the reality of the dissolution of sovereignty on the one hand and the necessity to solve global problems on the other, new forums of (conference) diplomacy were established and more international and supranational organizations created. The European Union (EU) is an excellent example. It possesses instruments that are normally only at the disposal of nation states. Nevertheless, in all matters that are of major concern for member states, the EU is guided by the intergovernmental working institutions. These mechanics have an impact on the diplomacy between the member states of the EU. The *European External Action Service* operates alongside the national foreign services and provides collective knowledge resources for the smaller member states in particular. Thus the need for global management has produced diplomacy and diplomats that represent their national interests and supranational aims at the same time.

Diplomacy can also be understood as the mediation of societies in a broad discourse[4] – not necessarily in a friendly conversation, but some-

---

4 A thought by Michael Koch, "Wozu noch Diplomaten?", in *Auswärtiges Amt: Diplomatie als Beruf*, ed. Enrico Brandt and Christian Buck (Opladen: Leske und Budrich, 2002), 350–59 (357).

times precisely the opposite. Whether it is the application of hard power, coercive measures, soft power, the power of institutions, or symbolic power, governments and other international interacting actors today feel obligated to explain their actions not only to their official dialogue partners, but also often to their own publics, as well as to non-state observers and actors outside their own borders. In his chapter *Hanns W. Maull* points out which dangers can arise, considering the technological advances and increasing expectations that could even lead to 'foreign policy autism.'

Contrary to the hopes of national-populist movements' that nation states will win back their former status as sovereign actors, in reality, the process of dissolution of physical and non-physical borders continues at great speed. While states attempt to preserve their formal status as the last legitimate source of national and international governmental leadership, avenues are opening up for non-diplomatic, internationally active governmental institution, parliaments, internationally active companies, media, non-governmental organizations, and organized crime. All of these attempt to influence a society or the community of states. *Karsten D. Voigt* analyses some of these processes in his chapter concerning the EU. Companies' interest in shaping conditions abroad leads them to use their leverage over governments, which in turn aim to attract investments and create new jobs. The politics of nominally sovereign states depend on a flow of activities, which are mostly subject to governmental control and which cross traditional borders. Official politics is reduced to attempts to manage the situations that result from incidents outside their sphere of influence. Political participation takes place across borders, and not only in times of crises and wars. The discourse about foreign policy amongst elites and publics dissolves its borders at the same time. Thus grey areas are created, which are concerned with foreign policy to varying degrees. Here, foreign ministries are hardly poised to moderate negotiations anymore. Diplomatic institutions are rather more like diplomacy's 'face' to the outside than actual movers of the world. The variety of elements of modern diplomatic activity creates a problem of coherence for diplomatic work in the foreign ministries and embassies. This difficulty is aggravated by the increasing number of 'attachés' of other governmental institutions, or institutions with their own agendas and priorities in the embassies. Diplomatic bodies, which are confronted with such difficult-to-control tasks, could be tempted to retreat to technocratic procedural modes and become content with working results that are just 'good enough.' As *Andrew Cooper* argues, the effort to avoid responsibility under the pressure of the latest developments could begin to drain sources of diplomatic strength and influence.

Presumably, civil society is only occasionally aware of the full impact of globalization on international events. However, once a public recognizes that impact, it demands foreign policy measures that are outside the range of political possibilities. Thus, not only politicians, but also diplomats are forced to suggest actions that promise satisfactory solutions to publics. At least modern conference diplomacy still succeeds in following Bismarck's notion and thus often manages to avoid conflicts for as long as possible. However, civil society or other actors regularly attempt to take things into their own hands – usually through the institutionalization and organization of publics. This sometimes makes it possible to accomplish aims that had been abandoned by traditional diplomacy. The achievements of the Paris Climate Conference in 2015, as *R. S. Zaharna* points out, would not have been possible (and the conference might not have taken place at all) without the lobbying of highly active NGOs, which worked together for a long period with politicians and diplomats. In turn, many of the UN's Sustainable Development Goals need the commitment of transnationally active companies.

However, civil society's demands may also be at the root of movements that do not help to solve global problems, but rather aggravate them. The anti-Islamic Pegida movement in Germany is one example. In many cases, however, the question of whether a civic movement has a positive or negative impact depends on the political attitude of the observer, as is the case in the conflict over the activities of foreign NGOs in China. Diplomacy, which adapts to this new reality, has to balance its own aims as the democratically legitimate representation of the overall population of a country with the individual interests of civic organizations. Through such endeavours, and confronted with more complex operative tasks and greater public expectations than ever before, diplomacy will be less administrative activity and more 'politics.' This means that publics will treat diplomacy as politics too – which can result in mistrust.

4. Global Aspects

Like any other form of governance, diplomacy strives to be successful. Its achievements are measured along predetermined guidelines and are judged on the value of the aims it achieved or failed to realize. Foreign policy can conceivably be successful despite diplomatic failures. The definition of diplomatic 'success' must therefore encompass global conditions and future prospects as well as management of expectations caused by international requirements. However, some parts of national publics still identify with the nation-states of the past. They expect successful foreign policy from their governments. They expect that they will be represented by them and accept that the representation of their interests may lead to substantial conflict with other nation-states. This dynamic can lead to a strong emotional impact by the governmental use of diplomatic instruments. *R. S. Zaharna* addresses emotionality as a determining dynamic element of foreign policy in her chapter. The problem here is the public's expectations directed at the nation-state conjoined with the need for the government to represent the interests of a nation in a world of interdependencies.

The question of whether the present societal and global changes will be the catalyst for homogenization or heterogenization of diplomacy remains unanswered in this volume. States learn from one another, and today they also learn from new international institutions. At the same time, their own intellectual traditions play an additional role. The United States and Europe are impacted by their adherence to various forms of market liberalism. In Russia and China the communist-led government traditionally influenced diplomacy through the principle of ideology over pragmatism. As *Kim B. Olsen* explains, having these various politico-economic heritages in mind, states (unaware of the influence of non-governmental actors in their national pursuit of transforming economic power into diplomatic influence) lack the fundamental understanding of today's geo-economic strains in diplomatic activity.

The role of diplomacy in the 21st century is less clearly defined than in the past. Its influence on the organization of the international order is decreasing. Diplomacy is caught in the continuous dispute between new technical demands and opportunities coupled with the expectations of new actors and publics as well as internal societal changes. At the same time, the diplomacy of a nation-state has to pursue, due to its traditional foreign policy pragmatic rationalism,[5] effective, efficient, and (legal as well as moral) legitimate strategies in the international environment. The question of a new normative framework for this kind of significantly changed diplomacy, and whether this is even possible, remains unanswered for the Working Group of the SWP. An answer will eventually be determined by whether the governmental activity of democracies can gain or reestablish the indispensable trust of citizens in the representative institutions of foreign policy.

5 See John Robert Kelley, "The New Diplomacy: Evolution of a Revolution", *Diplomacy & Statecraft* 21, no. 2 (June 2010): 286–305 (286).

Diplomats and the Use of Economic Sanctions

Sascha Lohmann

Diplomats have been closely involved in the threat and actual use of economic sanctions – a manifestation of the "capacity to interrupt commercial intercourse."[1] However, the central role of diplomats in wielding this particular instrument of economic force has not yet received systematic scrutiny. On the one hand, diplomatic practitioners usually deal with broader issues of war and peace in their autobiographical accounts, and, if they discuss particular cases in which they relied on economic sanctions as a means to extract concessions, they do so in a rather anecdotal fashion. On the other hand, scholars commonly employ various theoretical perspectives and empirical evidence in order to generalize across different contexts, thereby offering little practical insights into how to deal with concrete cases.

Equipped with only an impressionistic body of practical knowledge about the use of economic force, diplomats from the United States and the member states of the European Union (EU) are struggling to keep up with an increasing reliance on ever more sophisticated economic sanctions in the pursuit of national security and foreign policy objectives. Until now, there exists not a single official American or European doctrine that could provide guidance for the use of economic force. This lack of systematic thinking contrasts sharply with the elaborated military doctrines that lay out principles governing the use of armed force by specifying the triggering conditions, applicable procedures, and responsible actors tasked to carry it out. This intellectual imbalance can hardly be justified given that military and economic power occupy opposite sides of the same coin.[2] At a time when the selective and comprehensive imposition of trade as well as financial sanctions has emerged as the go-to option for decision-makers on both sides of the Atlantic, addressing a constantly growing number of per-

---

1 Robert Gilpin, *The Political Economy of International Relations* (Princeton, NJ: Princeton University Press, 1987), 76.

2 "Power is indivisible; and the military and economic weapons are merely different instruments of power." Edward H. Carr, *The Twenty Years' Crisis, 1919–1939: An Introduction to the Study of International Relations* (Edinburgh: R. & R. Clarke, 1946), 119.

ceived foreign policy and national security threats emanating from state and non-state actors alike, what has previously figured merely as a lamentable lacunae may soon turn into a strategic liability.

Against this backdrop, I assess the changing role of diplomats in the use of economic sanctions by drawing on empirical evidence from foreign and national security policy of the United States and the EU. This chapter proceeds as follows: in the first section, I briefly discuss the causes of the increasing prominence of the use of economic sanctions after World War II, and its adverse consequence of contributing to the side-lining of diplomats in contemporary diplomacy. In the second section, I briefly review how the existing political science literature has inadequately theorized the relationship between diplomats and the use of economic force. In the third section, I conclude by suggesting why the role of diplomats in the use of economic sanctions should be strengthened and offer some practical steps in that direction.

Progressing Practice

When conducting political intercourse beyond their borders, rulers had used economic sanctions to restrict trade and financial interactions well before the term *diplomacy* entered into the French and English dictionaries in the late 18th century.[3] Until the first half of the 20th century, these measures had overwhelmingly complemented the use of armed force among the consolidated political communities in North America and Europe, either in the form of land-based sieges or naval blockades.[4] Consequently, monitoring and enforcing the respective restrictions required physical inspection such as interdicting cargo transported via train or ships, a task carried out by members of the armed forces.[5] Diplomats came to replace soldiers as agents of the use of economic force when the newly created international institutions, first the League of Nations and later the United Nations, as well as individual nation states acting alone or together, gradually

3 Halvard Leira, "A Conceptual History of Diplomacy", in *The SAGE Handbook of Diplomacy*, ed. Costas M. Constantinou, Pauline Kerr and Paul Sharp (London: SAGE, 2016), 28–38.

4 "[T]he struggle to secure and deny supplies is a common feature of ancient as well as modern warfare." Michael Walzer, *Just and Unjust Wars: A Moral Argument with Historical Illustrations* (London: Allen Lane, 1977), 170.

5 Lance E. Davis and Stanley L. Engerman, *Naval Blockades in Peace and War: An Economic History since 1750* (Cambridge: Cambridge University Press, 2006).

substituted the use of armed force with that of economic force beginning in the second half of the 20th century.

Markets have become one of the main battlefields at the beginning of the 21st century.

This shift away from the use of armed to economic force was mainly driven by three technological and societal developments: firstly, the development of nuclear weapons led to a rapid decline of the utility of armed force, since its actual use among major powers would have assured their mutual destruction. Later on, armed force also turned out to be a rather blunt and therefore ineffective instrument to cope with unconventional threats posed by limited or collapsing statehood, transnational violent extremism, and organized crime. This is not to say that armed forced completely ceased to be used, as the continuation of covert operations and other types of limited use of armed force such as drones or cyber warfare amply demonstrates to this day. Secondly, the unilateral threat and actual use of armed force became morally shunned and legally relegated to being an *ultima ratio* that could be legitimately applied under the Charta of the United Nations only as a measure of self-defence or pursuant to a collective authorization by the Security Council. Finally, the use of economic sanctions was further elevated by the emergence of post-heroic societies across Western countries where the associated post-material values would henceforth provoke almost allergic reactions to casualties on the battlefield.[6] Without having to send troops into harm's way, the use of economic sanctions allows contemporary decision-makers in the United States and Europe to inflict equally substantial political and economic costs on adversaries in order to influence their decision-making. Due to its comparatively high utility vis-à-vis other policy instruments, the use of economic force has also frequently been applied by the Chinese and Russian governments.[7] Due to this change in the pattern of the application of force, markets have become one of the main battlefields at the beginning of the 21st century.[8]

---

6 Herfried Münkler, *Der Wandel des Krieges: Von der Symmetrie zur Asymmetrie* (Weilerswist: Velbrück Wissenschaft, 2006), 310–354.

7 William J. Norris, *Chinese Economic Statecraft: Commercial Actors, Grand Strategy, and State Control* (Ithaca, NY: Cornell University Press, 2016); Adam N. Stulberg, *Well-Oiled Diplomacy: Strategic Manipulation and Russia's Energy Statecraft in Eurasia* (Albany, NY: State University of New York Press, 2007).

8 Robert D. Blackwill and Jennifer M. Harris, *War by Other Means: Geoeconomics and Statecraft* (Cambridge, MA: The Belknap Press of Harvard University Press, 2016).

This shift in statecraft has been most pronounced in the United States; here the Department of the Treasury now occupies a central role in foreign policy and national security policy-making, overseeing a vast regime of unilateral economic sanctions employed against state and non-state actors around the world. Whereas the Department of State was instrumental in building strong financial and trade relationships with other nations and through international institutions after World War II, the Department of the Treasury has increasingly manipulated these relationships as a way to generate pressure on adversaries and allies alike. Within the Department of the Treasury, the Office of Foreign Assets Control (OFAC) is the lead agency that implements and enforces financial and trade sanctions under national emergency powers granted by Congress to the president pursuant to two key statutes: the *Trading with the Enemy Act of 1917* and the *International Emergency Economic Powers Act of 1977*. Every U.S. president since Franklin D. Roosevelt has utilized these economic sanctions to conduct U.S. foreign and national security policy. Under the George W. Bush administration, the use of financial sanctions was elevated to a primary instrument in the 'Global War on Terrorism.' At the same time, members of Congress re-inserted themselves into foreign policy-making by using economic sanctions as a legislative vehicle, forcing the administration's hand by broadening designation criteria and constraining executive power to lift and terminate the use of economic sanctions, as in the cases of Iran and Russia.

The increasing reliance on trade and financial sanctions elevated senior officials from the Department of the Treasury to pursue diplomatic missions to garner support for, and offer warnings about, non-compliance with unilateral U.S. economic sanctions in foreign capitals and corporate headquarters abroad.[9] These increasingly frequent missions further undermined the leadership position of diplomats in conducting U.S. foreign and national security policy. Whereas the threat of being side-lined by other bureaucratic and non-state actors in the conduct of diplomacy had been

9 Juan C. Zarate, *Treasury's War: The Unleashing a New Era of Financial Warfare* (New York: PublicAffairs, 2013). Previously, officials from finance ministries and especially central banks provided issue-specific expertise in multilateral negotiations over the provision of public goods through international institutions. Since the 1920s, it had been utilized by governments to deal with a growing number of topics. See Eric Helleiner, "Financial Officials as Diplomats: Evolving Issues, Actors, Techniques since the 1920s," in *The Oxford Handbook of Modern Diplomacy*, ed. Andrew F. Cooper, Jorge Heine and Ramesh Thakur (Oxford: Oxford University Press, 2013), 160–75.

feared by diplomats in the past, the current marginalization of the Department of State is truly unprecedented.[10] Although less pronounced, the side-lining of diplomats also takes place within the EU, where an equally increasing use of economic sanctions is ultimately decided by the heads of governments in the European Council and eventually implemented by bureaucrats in the European Commission and national governments, with diplomats playing mainly a supportive role at both stages of the policy circle. As a matter of fact, the ever-growing importance of the EU's 'restrictive measures' over the last two decades in furthering the objectives of its Common Foreign and Security Policy has not been matched by the number of diplomats working in the Sanctions Unit of the European External Action Service. Given the encroachment of other bureaucratic actors on diplomats' traditional prerogative to conduct foreign affairs, it was no coincidence that mostly economic and finance ministers were in attendance when the United Nations Security Council adopted Resolution 2253 on December 17, 2015, which added the *Islamic State in Iraq and the Levant* (ISIS) to the existing multilateral financial sanctions regime against *Al-Qaeda*.

Trailing Theory

The soaring use of economic sanctions by U.S. and EU decision-makers to pursue a growing number of foreign and national security objectives correspondingly required expertise about how financial markets and the global trading system function. This expertise mostly resided in finance or trade ministries, central banks, and the private sector. In the United States, the demand for this specialized economic knowledge has been supplied and operationalized by a new bureaucratic cast whose members are neither diplomats nor soldiers. Notwithstanding, they take on tasks that used to be assigned exclusively to diplomats, such as negotiating with foreign governments and their home companies about cooperating on the design, implementation and enforcement of economic sanctions. In doing so, its members have directly targeted state and non-state adversaries and their respective supporters since the early 1990s, engaging in what can be described as

10 Dean Acheson, "The Eclipse of the State Department", *Foreign Affairs* 49, no. 4 (July 1971): 593–606; George F. Kennan, "Diplomacy without Diplomats?", *Foreign Affairs* 76, no. 5 (March 1997): 198–212; Ronan Farrow, *War on Peace: The End of Diplomacy and the Decline of American Influence* (New York: W. W. Norton & Company, 2018).

economic warfare without an official declaration of war.[11] The members of this new bureaucratic cast can accordingly be described as financial warriors.

The rise of these financial warriors has so far only been documented in autobiographical accounts of former protagonists.[12] This development has otherwise gone largely unnoticed in the existing literature on diplomacy and economic sanctions. One reason for this could be the persistent misconception by practitioners and scholars of international relations that economics would pertain to 'low' politics while the conduct of foreign and national security policy would occupy the throne of 'high' politics, the latter thought to be firmly in the hands of diplomats. This questionable analytical separation between 'low' and 'high' politics might be a path-dependent result of the disdain for economic issues that had featured prominently during the 19th century among the diplomatic corps. Traditionally, its members were mainly comprised of aristocrats who viewed the emancipation of the merchant middle class with utter disdain.[13] Alternatively, this analytical separation might also be a consequence of the dominance of the liberal school of thought in the academic study of economics and politics, and the apparent contradiction posed by the use of economic sanctions, which violates two of its basic premises: firstly, that markets operate independently from state interference, and secondly that economic interdependence reduces conflict. Having dethroned mercantilism as a dominant paradigm of international political economy, liberal ideas exerted a lasting impact on decision-makers, as evidenced in the words of former U.S. Secretary of State Cordell Hull, who proclaimed that "if trade crosses borders, soldiers won't." Regardless of its cause, the analytical separation of suppos-

---

11 Keith Kendrick, "In Economic Battle, Soldiers Fight on Carpet", *The Washington Post*, 19 September 1990, https://www.washingtonpost.com/archive/politics/1990/09/19/in-economic-battle-soldiers-fight-on-carpet/1c39d1e6-93c8-43aa-a129-eec28d15fe83/?noredirect=on&utm_term=.2f43f51e7abd (accessed 18 July 2018).

12 John B. Taylor, *Global Financial Warriors: The Untold Story of International Finance in the Post 9/11 World* (New York: W. W. Norton & Company, 2007); Orde F. Kittrie, "New Sanctions for a New Century: Treasury's Innovative Use of Financial Sanctions", *University of Pennsylvania Journal of International Law* 30, no. 3 (Spring 2009): 789–822; Juan C. Zarate, "Harnessing the Financial Furies: Smart Financial Power and National Security", *The Washington Quarterly* 32, no. 4 (2009): 43–59. For a critique see Ibrahim Warde, *The Price of Fear: Al-Qaeda and the Truth behind the Financial War on Terror* (London: I. B. Tauris, 2007), 14.

13 As the prime example of the low regard for economics vis-à-vis the 'high' politics involving war and peace, see Werner Sombart, *Händler und Helden: Patriotische Besinnungen* (München: Duncker & Humblot, 1915).

edly low and high politics in the study of international relations and diplomacy runs contrary to empirical evidence. In particular, the use of economic sanctions stretches back as far as the city states of ancient Greece. Later, economics and diplomacy evolved hand-in-hand as foreign trade missions were both causes and consequences of the establishment of official diplomatic ties among governments throughout the 18th and 19th centuries.

In the past, scholarship overwhelmingly neglected the economic means available to diplomats. Instead, scholars extensively scrutinized the intimate involvement of diplomats in the use of armed force (what Carl von Clausewitz had called the 'other means' and what its academic acolytes nowadays discuss as 'coercive diplomacy').[14] Some scholars working in the sub-discipline of Diplomatic Studies have recently begun to theorize the economic ends of foreign and national security policy as "economic diplomacy."[15] This rather blurry concept encompasses myriad efforts, sometimes also labelled commercial or trade diplomacy, which relate to the promotion and support of business interests abroad, the negotiation of trade agreements and international institutions of economic governance,[16] as

---

14 Thomas C. Schelling, *Arms and Influence* (New Haven, CT: Yale University Press, 1966), 3; Alexander L. George, *Forceful Persuasion: Coercive Diplomacy as an Alternative to War* (Washington, D.C.: United States Institute of Peace Press, 1991); Alexander L. George and William E. Simons, eds., *The Limits of Coercive Diplomacy*, 2nd ed. (Boulder: Westview Press, 1994); Christer Jönsson, "Diplomacy", in *Encyclopedia of Power*, ed. Keith M. Dowding (Thousand Oaks, CA: SAGE, 2011), 188–90; Peter Viggo Jakobsen, "Coercive Diplomacy", in *The SAGE Handbook of Diplomacy*, ed. Constantinou, Kerr and Sharp (see note 3), 476–86; Tarak Barkawi, "Diplomacy, War, and World Politics", in *Diplomacy and the Making of World Politics*, ed. Ole Jacob Sending, Vincent Pouliot and Iver B. Neumann (Cambridge: Cambridge University Press, 2015), pp. 55–79.

15 Maaike Okano-Heijmans, "Conceptualizing Economic Diplomacy: The Crossroads of International Relations, Economics, IPE and Diplomatic Studies", *The Hague Journal of Diplomacy* 6, no. 1–2 (January 2011): 7–36; Idem, "Economic Diplomacy", in *The SAGE Handbook of Diplomacy*, ed. Constantinou, Kerr and Sharp (see note 3), 552–63. For an early effort, see John Pinder, "Economic Diplomacy", in *World Politics: An Introduction*, ed. James N. Rosenau, Kenneth W. Thompson and Gavin Boyd (New York: Free Press, 1976), 312–36.

16 Leonard Seabrooke, "Economists and Diplomacy: Professions and the Practice of Economic Policy", *International Journal* 66, no. 3 (September 2011): 629–42 (641); Idem, "Diplomacy as Economic Consultancy", in *Diplomacy and the Making of World Politics*, ed. Sending, Pouliot and Neumann(see note 14), 195–219.

well as foreign aid and other types of monetary assistance.[17] However, this literature largely neglects the economic means available to diplomats in the pursuit of foreign policy and national security objectives.[18]

While the theory of power under the condition of economic interdependence has been a central theme of the realist school of thought,[19] we still lack systematic inquiries into the use of economic force by diplomats. David A. Baldwin came fairly close, although he ultimately shied away from connecting his seminal analytical framework of economic statecraft to the particular role of diplomats, arguing that such a move "broadens the concept of 'diplomacy' so much that it makes it difficult to think in terms of diplomatic alternatives to economic techniques."[20] This proves to be highly unfortunate as his book has significantly improved our thinking about the possibilities and pitfalls of the use of economic sanctions.

Bridging the Gap

In order to demonstrate their continuing relevance for diplomacy in the 21st century, diplomats need to come to terms with the profound shift from the use of armed to economic force, which is threatening to further side-line them vis-à-vis other bureaucratic actors in the implementation of foreign and national security policy in the United States and the member states of the EU. Due to their vast body of specialized and general knowledge, acquired through systematic education and training, diplomats must

17 Donna Lee, "The Growing Influence of Business in U.K. Diplomacy", *International Studies Perspectives* 5, no. 1 (February 2004): 50–54; Donna Lee and David Hudson, "The Old and New Significance of Political Economy in Diplomacy", *Review of International Studies* 30, no. 3 (July 2004): 343–60; Paul Sharp, *Diplomatic Theory of International Relations* (Cambridge: Cambridge University Press, 2009), 222–42; Olivier Naray, "Commercial Diplomacy: An Integrative Framework", *International Journal of Diplomacy and Economy* 1, no. 2 (2012): 119–33.

18 Nicholas Bayne and Stephen Woolcock, "What Is Economic Diplomacy?", in *The New Economic Diplomacy: Decision-Making and Negotiation in International Economic Relations*, ed. Nicholas Bayne and Stephen Woolcock, 4th ed. (Abingdon: Routledge, 2016), 1–15 (2–5).

19 Jonathan Kirshner, "The Political Economy of Realism", in: *Unipolar Politics: Realism and State Strategies after the Cold War*, ed. Ethan Kapstein and Michael Mastanduno (New York: Columbia University Press, 1999), 88–102; Rawi Abdelal and Jonathan Kirshner, "Strategy, Economic Relations, and the Definition of National Interests", *Security Studies* 9, no. 1 (1999): 123–62.

20 David A. Baldwin, *Economic Statecraft* (Princeton, NJ: Princeton University Press, 1985), 35.

continue to play a central role in the design, implementation, and enforcement of economic sanctions. Although there exists neither an agreed-upon epistemic canon within the sphere of public policy of what economic statecraft entails, nor is there an institutionalized structure in most Western countries geared to facilitating its most effective application, admittedly diplomats are uniquely suited to act as primary agents of the use of economic sanctions. This is because of their ability to weigh competing policy objectives in the pursuit of diplomacy, according to their short- and long-term implications. Their comprehensive view, grounded in profound contextual knowledge gained through constant exposure to different cultural conditions, distinguishes them from their colleagues in financial and trade ministries who tend to myopically pursue narrower policy objectives. With respect to the use of economic sanctions, this may entail increasing economic pressure and ensuring universal compliance by rigorous enforcement without considering what exactly the other sides want and why. As Sir Robert F. Cooper has pointed out, "Diplomacy is partly Newtonian physics – power, pressure and leverage – but it is also about what people want."[21] Thus, the benefit of diplomacy sometimes may be to buy additional time for negotiations and for necessary social change to happen.

A second career path with a focus on specialized training for tasks such as designing and implementing trade and financial sanctions could be a viable solution.

In order to strengthen their role in the use of economic sanctions, especially within governments of EU member states and particularly in Germany, the career path of diplomats should not only lead to the education of generalists who can adapt to any task. The current practice of having the entire diplomatic corps rotate mandatorily for fixed terms creates immense opportunity costs because individual diplomats must acquire the highly technical knowledge required for the use of economic sanctions at every turn. Instead, a second career path with a focus on specialized training for highly specific tasks such as designing and implementing trade and financial sanctions could be a viable solution. In the United States, former Secretary of State Hillary Rodham Clinton initiated similar steps as part of her *Economic Statecraft Initiative* between late 2011 and 2012. Although receiving only scant attention at the time, her initiative lead to lasting organizational

21 Robert Cooper, "Ukraine and Iran Vindicate Ashton's Deft Diplomacy", *Financial Times*, 12 December 2013, https://www.ft.com/content/a4baf248-5ea9-11e3-8621-00144feabdc0 (accessed 18 July 2018).

changes within the bureaucracy of the Department of State, which were based on an appreciation of the crucial role of economic force for U.S. diplomacy.[22] As specialists on the use of economic force, diplomats could become orchestrators directing other bureaucratic actors within their own governments to contribute the requisite specialized knowledge, instead of being sidelined by them in the pursuit of diplomacy.

22 Hillary R. Clinton, "Economic Statecraft", Speech at the Economic Club of New York, New York City, 14 October 2011, https://2009-2017.state.gov/secretary/20092013clinton/rm/2011/10/175552.htm (accessed 24 July 2018).

Populism and the Domestic Challenge to Diplomacy

Andrew Cooper

The challenge to diplomacy for numerous Western countries has become domestic in nature. Although serious tensions exist concerning the global institutional architecture, these do not constitute the existential threat of the 1930s. Unlike in that earlier era, there has been no outright abandonment of international organizations (IOs), as punctuated by the failure of the League of Nations. Rather than disappearing, IOs have proliferated, albeit with a bias towards informal self-selected forums including the G20 and the Financial Stability Board. Nor does the world's geo-political environment include a cluster of totalitarian states bent on territorial expansion by military means. In many ways, liberal internationalism continues to hold sway, at least as judged by the degree of complex interdependence. Instead of the hold of autarchy (with large national champions having exclusive authority in zones of control), it is the image of hyper-globalization that defines the 21st century. Massive corporations are not the only victors from this situation, since large NGOs (Oxfam, MSF) and philanthropic bodies (The Gates Foundation) have benefited as well. Moreover, reflecting this kind of pluralism, it is no longer a hegemonic or unipolar era. Rather there is ample space particularly for big state actors beyond the West (above all the BRICS, including China, India, Brazil, and South Africa as well as Russia) and outside the traditional establishment of the G7/8 to exert influence. Indeed, at the recent 2018 BRICS summit in Johannesburg, the BRICS positioned themselves as defenders of the multilateral economic order.

At the core of the current dilemma is not whether diplomacy (and diplomats situated in foreign ministries) is in the process of disappearing on the global stage but rather that these forms of institution and machinery are contested and stigmatized domestically by populist forces. Akin to the challenge confronting other institutions, diplomacy is viewed as being a constraining instrument, part of a self-serving and controlling establishment. From the theoretical tradition associated with Ernesto Laclau,[1] the

1 Ernesto Lacula, "Populism: What's in a Name?", in *Populism and the Mirror of Democracy*, ed. Francisco Panizza (London: Verso, 2005), 32–49.

populist logic may be contrasted with nationalists in one fundamental dimension. Whereas nationalists differentiate horizontally between those in and outside (the other) the nation state, populists differentiate on a down/up basis with antagonism between the elite and 'the people' as underdog.

This anti-diplomatic/foreign ministry sentiment is most noticeable in the Brexit campaign with its aversion to insiders and communities of sentiment and interest beyond the national. However, this type of contestation can be located in multiple sites beyond the UK as well. In various sections of the European populist movements, forces rail against considerations of diplomatic solidarity, above all on the migration issue. On top of all this, of course, is the concerted challenge to contemporary diplomatic culture that U.S. President Donald Trump presents. On one level, to be sure, Trump can be depicted as a return to an older type of diplomacy. Privileging ad hoc processes as a means to circumvent all forms of institutionalization whether formal (UN, IFIs, WTO, NATO) or informal (G20, contact groups etc.). On another level, the operational style of President Trump is focused on personalism, detachment from any fixed ideology, a winner take-it all approach to negotiations, the use of bilateral one-on-ones, constant surprises, and direct communication with 'his' supporters combined with an erratic use of Twitter

Thus this accumulated challenge to diplomacy and foreign ministries in particular comes not from the periphery of the global system where it might be expected. After all, small states were among those that experienced the heaviest diplomatic casualties of the global financial crisis. Additionally, small states have been left out of the new institutions, not only in terms of the G20 but also the BRICS-states and the MIKTA[2] partnership. Furthermore, space for normatively driven diplomatic initiatives, which was led in some considerable part by small states, for example at the International Court, has been curtailed.

That the contested view of diplomacy and diplomats is most robust in countries at the core of the international system, is a dynamic that can only be understood in the context of a backlash against a wider segment of established institutional culture. Such an adverse reaction at least to some degree reflects the ascendancy of celebrity culture, which puts the onus on personalistic spectacle rather than a culture of achievement. What is new

2 BRICS refers to Brazil, Russia, India, China and South Africa, while MIKTA is an informal partnership between Mexico, Indonesia, the Republic of Korea, Turkey and Australia.

and different is the connection between celebrity status and populism rather than an institutional connection. Whereas celebrities such as George Clooney, Angelina Jolie, or for that matter, Bill Gates or Ted Turner, were associated with the United Nations and/or global initiatives aimed at delivering global public goods,[3] celebrity politicians, notably Donald Trump – or indeed Boris Johnson and Beppe Grillo (the former leader of the Five Star Movement in Italy, who focused internally to appeal to large domestic constituencies) – are closer connected with populism.

Foreign ministries have become more fragile in their standing across a wide spectrum of countries. The view that diplomats/foreign service officers have a unique ability to interpret the national interest is strongly embedded, accentuated by the legacy of a distinctive culture that highlights the separation of diplomats not only from other components of governmental bureaucracy but citizens at large. Diplomacy evolved to "function [as intermediator] between states and societies separated by institutions, law, culture, economics, and language."[4] Therefore, as long as foreign ministries had a special status (with the ability to some considerable extent to act as the primary conduit for external relations) the 'guild' system vis-à-vis diplomacy imparted some considerable strengths. However, increasingly stirred up and mobilized citizens push to circumvent this component of the establishment, as they also do in the contest between representative and participatory democracy.

Through this type of framework, therefore, it is not surprising that diplomacy and diplomats have faced challenges of even a more formidable nature beyond the West when a combination of celebrity status and populism completely captures a state. Venezuela under President Hugo Chávez (1999–2013) fits this model with its mixture of charismatic leadership and so-called 'diplomacy of the peoples' *(diplomacia de los pueblos)*. According to Cardozo the deterioration of professional diplomacy in favor of personal relations and the "diplomacy of microphones" meshed with the "definition of diplomacy in terms of support for the regime",[5] rather than having any professional basis. As Serbin and Serbin Pont put it:

---

3 Andrew F. Cooper, *Celebrity Diplomacy* (Boulder, CO: Paradigm Publishers, 2007).

4 Georg Haynal, *DOA: Diplomacy on the Ascendant in the Age of Disintermediation* (Cambridge, MA: Weatherhead Center for International Affairs, Harvard University, 2002), https://programs.wcfia.harvard.edu/files/fellows/files/haynal.pdf? m=1357 530295 (accessed 7 May 2018).

5 Elsa Cardozo, "La política exterior del gobierno bolivariano y sus implicaciones en el plano doméstico", Caracas: Instituto Latinoamericano de Investigaciones Sociales

"The Foreign Service was restructured in 2000 and 2005. Changes included the modification of the Pedro Gual diplomatic academy so that professionals entering the diplomatic service would also have to do social service and experience personally the structure of the Bolivarian social missions and to acknowledge their effects on the revolution."[6]

The populist challenge highlights the disconnection between a perceived entrenched elite and 'the people' embracing hyper-empowered individuals as their champions. Personalism is no longer restricted to the leaders of distinctive political parties. The cult of celebrity owes no loyalty to established patterns of performance. Even the most cynical citizens are drawn to the aura of autonomous individuals who are the contradistinction of what diplomatic culture represents.

Making the challenge even more formidable is the ability of these hyper-empowered individuals to represent themselves as flag bearers for the frustrations of ordinary citizens. They operate through loose networking as outsiders rather than using the closed clubs of insiders. All of this is not to say that the backlash extended through the process of disintermediation dismisses all diplomacy and diplomats as not fit for purpose. On the contrary, what stands out is the contrast between the generalized contestation of diplomacy and the high value placed on specific diplomats, as witnessed by the tributes to Ambassador Chris Stevens and others killed in the 2012 Benghazi attack. In the UK, it is an open question whether attacks on diplomacy by populist politicians such as Nigel Farage are authentic or simply a response to the willingness of some diplomats such as Sir Ivan Rogers to speak 'truth to power' about Brexit. After all, Farage revelled in meeting Trump in an unofficial capacity, particularly as the idea was floated by Trump that Farage would make a 'great' British ambassador to the United States.

Even with these caveats, nonetheless, the challenge to diplomacy and foreign ministries is a serious one. Given the power of the disintermediation, an opportunistic set of ascendant political leaders – even those located at the core of the international system – have considerable incentive to diminish 'their' own diplomats as part of a wider campaign to stigmatize the traditional establishment.

(ILDIS), Oficina en Venezuela de la Fundación Friedrich Ebert, August 2010, 3–4, http://library.fes.de/pdf-files/bueros/caracas/08796.pdf (accessed 8 August 2018).

6 Andrés Serbin and Andrei Serbin Pont, "The Foreign Policy of the Bolivarian Republic of Venezuela: The Role and Legacy of Hugo Chávez", *Latin American Policy* 8, no. 2 (December 2017): 232–48.

Under this intense pressure there is a logic in diplomats demonstrating their value. Some modes of operation could well be downplayed in this process: for example, the high-profile efforts of ambassadors and missions to engage in public campaigns to criticize or even destabilize autocratic regimes. The efforts of Michael McFaul, the then U.S. Ambassador to Russia (2012–2014), on Twitter with a following of 60,000, falls into this category. So does the effort of U.S. Ambassador Robert Ford to Syria, who was already reaching out in 2011 (at the beginning of the Syrian crisis) to opposition forces and who visited cities under siege by the Assad government's security forces.

Facing the challenge of populism, diplomacy and diplomats need to be far more reactive. In these disruptive times, the most instrumentally attractive approach is one in which the institutions and machinery of diplomacy are geared towards delivery in the service of citizens. Again, this is not a completely novel strategy, but it is one that needs to be implanted into the mantra of 'public' diplomacy directed domestically. At every opportunity diplomacy and diplomats should counter the image of 'denationalis[ation]' – originally put forward as a concern by Sir Harold Nicolson in the inter-war years;[7] but it is a concept which under current turbulent conditions must return to the fore of thinking and practice.

7 See Derek Drinkwater, *Sir Harold Nicolson and International Relations* (Oxford: Oxford University Press, 2005).

Diplomatic Representation: States and Beyond

Christer Jönsson

Representation, in terms of standing and acting for others, is a core function of diplomacy. Historically, diplomats represented individual rulers; today they represent states. Their representative role hinges on the predominance of states in international relations.

> "When states become weaker, so do those who represent and derive authority from them. As the trend continues towards global decision-making for the big global issues on the one hand, and greater localisation and individualisation on the other, where does a state's representative fit in?"[1]

Representing states diplomatically in the 21st century is far from unproblematic. In the first part of this chapter, I will attempt to identify some contemporary and future challenging issues of state representation through diplomats. Moreover, in the 21st century actors other than states make claims to diplomatic representation. The second part of my chapter will therefore discuss the implications and challenges of broader diplomatic representation.

State Representation

From Antiquity to the Middle Ages, diplomats represented sovereign rulers in the sense that they were perceived to embody their sovereigns when they presented themselves at foreign courts. While such a view is alien to modern thought, today's principle of diplomatic immunity has deep roots in notions of personal representation. Early envoys were inviolable for the reason that they were to be treated "as though the sovereign himself were there."[2] Today, the status of diplomatic representatives, standing for some-

---

1 Tom Fletcher, *The Naked Diplomat: Power and Statecraft in the Digital Century* (London: William Collins, 2016), 14.

2 Grant V. McClanahan, *Diplomatic Immunity: Principles, Practices, Problems* (London: Hurst, 1989), 28.

one or something other, is understood as symbolic representation. The diplomat is then a representative in the same sense that a flag represents a nation.

Representation implies not only status (standing for others) but also behaviour (acting for others). Economists and political scientists analyse such relationships between representatives and those represented in terms of *principals* and *agents*. Principal-agent relations arise whenever one party (principal) delegates certain tasks to another party (agent). Diplomats and elected politicians are obvious examples of agents, who have been entrusted with certain tasks from their principals (governments/voters). Due to conflicting preferences and information asymmetry, agents may pursue other interests than those of the principal. Delegation is therefore usually combined with control mechanisms, such as monitoring and audits.

The proper behaviour of a representative is a matter of intense debate, especially in the literature on representative democracy. At issue is whether agents have an "imperative mandate", being strictly accountable to their principals, or a "free mandate", being authorized to act on behalf of their principals.[3] It implies an appraisal of whether accountability or authorization is the key term to characterize the relationship between representatives and principals.

At first sight, diplomats as civil servants would seem to have a restricted or 'imperative' mandate compared to the freer mandate of elected politicians. However, this is a simplification. While varying in restrictions, the instructions and bargaining mandate of diplomats often allow room for initiative within the given frames. Diplomatic representation rests on two-way communication and mutual influence. Using their diplomatic talent in interaction with their own foreign ministry, diplomats have influence over the instructions they receive which may give them considerable leeway.

In short, standing and acting for others entails perennial dilemmas and issues concerning diplomats' symbolic role and the balancing act between the imperative and free mandate extremes. Are there, then, specific issues of diplomatic representation in the 21st century? Hereafter, I will identify some changes and trends, and raise questions concerning their implications. As for symbolic representation, I will discuss the change from immunity to vulnerability and the question of whether diplomats ought to mir-

3 Marek Sobolewski, "Electors and Representatives: A Contribution to the Theory of Representation", in *Representation*, ed. J. Roland Pennock and John W. Chapman (New York: Atherton Press, 1968), 95–107 (96).

ror the society they represent. In addition, I will identify three interrelated issues concerning principal-agent relations and diplomatic behaviour: what are the significant differences in representing a democratic or an authoritarian state? How can diplomats represent divided societies? And what problems are associated with representing a populist regime?

From Immunity to Vulnerability

For centuries, the fact that diplomats represented venerable principals – from powerful monarchs to established states – guaranteed their protected and privileged status. Whereas long-standing rules of diplomatic immunity and privileges by and large continue to be upheld in interstate relations, popular perceptions of diplomats have changed in recent decades. To the extent that diplomats are perceived as symbols of disliked countries, religions or '-isms', the quality of standing for others has been transformed from a rationale for diplomatic immunity to a rationale for political violence. No longer being inviolable symbols, diplomatic representatives have increasingly become highly vulnerable symbols.

In a polarized world diplomats and diplomatic facilities have become soft targets for terrorist attacks. For instance, of all terrorist attacks targeting the United States between 1969 and 2009, 28 percent were directly against U.S. diplomatic officers. In 2012 alone there were 95 attacks against various diplomatic institutions, of which more than one-third targeted UN personnel.[4] As a consequence, embassy security has become an overriding concern. Some embassies today have the appearance of fortresses or penitentiaries, with barbed wire atop and alongside high walls without windows. CCTV surveillance, turnstiles, metal detectors and crash proof barriers are only a few examples of security devices at embassies and consulates. One veteran U.S. diplomat speaks of "creeping militarization", as embassy security has become influenced by military priorities and requirements.[5] The military connection is also reflected in the fact that embassies and diplomats representing governments with ongoing military operations are particularly vulnerable.

---

4 Muhammad-Basheer A. Ismail, *Islamic Law and Transnational Diplomatic Law* (New York: Palgrave Macmillan, 2016), 139.

5 James L. Bullock, "Keeping Embassy Security in Perspective", *The Foreign Service Journal* 92, no. 4 (May 2015): 33–38, http://www.afsa.org/keeping-embassy-security-perspective (accessed 25 March 2018).

This raises the question of whether there are non-militarized approaches to restoring the protection and security of diplomats that have been a hallmark of diplomacy throughout centuries. The tendency toward increasing insecurity and vulnerability not only impedes diplomatic tasks but also threatens to render the recruitment process of qualified personnel more difficult.

Mirroring Society

Standing for others can be understood in another, more literal, sense. To what extent do diplomats need to mirror the social and ethnic composition of the societies they represent? For most of recorded history, diplomatic envoys have represented individual rulers rather than whole communities and have not necessarily come from the same country as their rulers. Well into the 19th century diplomats were aristocrats, who could easily change from one monarchical employer to another. The idea that diplomats should be an accurate reflection or typical of the society they represent is quite recent. With increasing migration, many – if not most – states will have a multiethnic and multicultural character in the 21st century. In countries with substantial immigration, such as Sweden, governments have recently made efforts to influence recruitment policies in such a way that diplomatic corps better mirror the multiethnic character of these societies.

The standard objection to taking measures to safeguard representativeness in this sense is that diplomats are supposed to represent national policies and values rather than the social and ethnic composition of the society they come from. However, the question needs to be raised how important the symbolic value of accurately reflecting their society might be in the perceptions of relevant audiences. Another consideration concerns the potential value of individuals with multiple cultural backgrounds and understandings in diplomatic negotiations with relevant counterparts. For instance, could diplomats recruited from the Muslim population in Germany or Sweden play a constructive role in negotiations with Arab countries?

Gender is another debated dimension of representativeness. In many diplomatic establishments around the world there is an ongoing quest to end formal and informal barriers and bring about gender parity, which will no doubt pervade the 21st century. Despite positive developments in recent years, diplomatic infrastructures still tend toward masculinized norms, homo-social environments and gendered divisions of labour.[6]

Democratic vs. Authoritarian States as Principals

The nature of the principal is one important factor determining the nature of diplomatic representation. Specifically, it matters whether the diplomatic agent has a single principal or receives instructions from a collective body. Principal-agent theory heeds the problems of collective or multiple principals, peculiarly to the increased autonomy agents may enjoy as a result of competing preferences among principals. The unequivocal instructions from a single sovereign in earlier times left less leeway for diplomats than the frequently vague instructions resulting from negotiations among different actors and agencies in modern democracies. And whereas democratic states place diplomats at the end of multiple chains of principals and agents, diplomats representing contemporary authoritarian states, with one clearly identifiable principal, have more restrictive mandates.

The changing balance between democratic and authoritarian states in the 21st century constitutes quite a change from the optimistic predictions of the final victory of liberal democracies after the end of the Cold War. This ought to make us think harder about differing parameters of diplomatic representation between democracies and autocracies and what consequences these might have. For instance, democratic methods of arriving at agreement by civilized discussion rather than coercive dictation have a bearing on diplomacy as well. The use of digital platforms by autocracies for info warfare represents a new facet of 21st century diplomacy. On the other hand, digital diplomacy offers an effective tool for democratic states to bypass the controlled media in authoritarian states.[7]

6 See Karin Aggestam and Ann E. Towns, eds., *Gendering Diplomacy and International Negotiation* (Basingstoke: Palgrave Macmillan, 2018).

7 Eytan Gilboa, "Digital Diplomacy", in *The SAGE Handbook of Diplomacy*, ed. Costas M. Constantinou, Pauline Kerr and Paul Sharp (London: Sage, 2016), 540–51 (542).

Representing Divided Societies

A specific case of representation dilemmas in the 21st century occur in divided societies. Two prominent examples are Great Britain after the Brexit referendum and the United States after the election of Donald Trump as president. These countries are politically split into two halves of similar strength, with opposing views on issues that diplomats have to deal with. On the one hand, this would seem to grant diplomats more leeway. But, on the other hand, the lack of firm and consistent policies, standpoints and instructions complicates life for diplomats significantly.

The lack of a firm consensus can be a serious liability in international negotiations, as the other side may try to exploit internal divisions and opposing standpoints. One common dynamic, well-known from repeated Cold War occurrences, is that hard-liners of both sides tend to reinforce each other's position. The Brexit negotiations will be a significant test case for whether old patterns hold in the new 21st century environment. This unique situation of an encounter between a deeply divided society and a coalition of a large number of dissimilar states makes for interesting observations concerning representation in the contemporary world.

Representing Populist Regimes

Another specific difficulty concerns the rise of populist regimes. Populism yields a democratic representation problem. Populists claim to represent 'the real people' or 'the silent majority.' By implication, those who do not share the populists' views and notion of 'the people' are not legitimate members of society. Populism is essentially anti-pluralist, which is in contradiction to the norm of coexistence – to 'live and let live' – on which both democracy and diplomacy rest.

The controversial conception of democratic representation domestically translates into an external diplomatic representation problem. Exploiting growing mistrust and suspicion among voters, populist leaders target diffuse and undefined forces, such as 'the establishment' or 'experts' who have ostensibly undermined the democratic system. Along with journalists, diplomats are typically included in these categories. The fact that xenophobia is often a component of populism does not make the situation easier for diplomats. This raises the question of how to represent a principal who distrusts you. The U.S. under President Trump is a case in point. The president has openly declared his lack of confidence in the State Department and his budget proposal for 2018 cuts its budget significantly. Furthermore, a number of important ambassadorial appointments have been postponed including countries such as Mexico, Saudi Arabia and Turkey. Among U.S. diplomats there is widespread distress, and many have chosen to leave the service.

As this current example illustrates, the problem of representing populist regimes is interrelated to the issue of differing principal-agent interests as well as the difficulty of representing divided societies.

Non-State Representation

Diplomatic recognition is a "ticket of general admission to the international arena",[8] which has been granted to states or state-like entities, and not to other influential international entities, such as multinational corporations or financial actors. Will the state-centric pattern of diplomatic recognition and representation persist in the 21st century, or are there signs of potential change?

One recent noteworthy exception to the state-centred pattern is the recognition of the EU as a diplomatic *persona*. This raises the question of whether this 'supranational challenge' heralds the introduction of other regional organizations on the diplomatic arena. Insofar as cities are increasingly making claims to becoming represented in the international arena, one may speak of a 'subnational challenge' as well. Most important, however, is the 'transnational challenge' from organizations and groups which act beyond national borders yet are not controlled by governments.

Supranational Representation

The EU is the prime example of a supranational actor in today's world. With the entry into force of the Lisbon Treaty in December 2009 the EU as such, not just the Commission, acquired a diplomatic *persona*. The EU 'foreign minister', the High Representative for Foreign Affairs and Security Policy, is assisted by the European External Action Service (EEAS). The recruitment process has not been unproblematic. Some 1,600 officials were transferred to the EEAS from the Commission and the Council Secretariat on 1 January, 2011. In addition, staffs are recruited among member-state

8 Stephen D. Krasner, *Sovereignty: Organized Hypocrisy* (Princeton, NJ: Princeton University Press, 1999), 16.

diplomats. The representational function of EU delegations is well established and EU diplomats take an active part in the local *corps diplomatique*. Yet several organizational questions are yet to be solved.[9]

One set of challenges concerns the 'double-hatted' character that the service shares with its foreign minister. Sceptics wonder how the two sets of career streams in the Commission and the Council Secretariat can be fused. Additionally, the recruitment of member-state diplomats adds to the heterogeneity and potential tensions. Another problematic aspect of supranational European diplomacy concerns the persistence of traditional, national diplomatic representation among the member states. The emergence of the EU as a diplomatic *persona* has not replaced, but merely added a new layer to, traditional diplomacy. To represent a conglomerate of states, which all have individual diplomatic representation, is no easy matter. Nor are there indications that other supranational entities than the EU will be granted similar diplomatic status and representation in the foreseeable future.

Subnational Representation

Traditional diplomacy presupposes centralized control of interaction across state boundaries. Regions and cities are then not recognized as diplomatic *personae* with representation of their own. Nor are constituent states in federal governments. However, there is an increased activity of subnational units. To refer to these cross-border activities sometimes the terms 'micro-diplomacy' and 'para-diplomacy' are sometimes used.

Today, some authors speak of a renaissance of cities as international actors.[10] The "governments of large cities and urban areas increasingly engage directly in diplomatic activities, opening representative offices in foreign capitals and other major world cities and sending their mayors on ev-

9 See Joachim A. Koops and Gjovalin Macaj, eds., *The European Union as a Diplomatic Actor* (Basingstoke: Palgrave Macmillan, 2015); Petar Petrov, Karolina Pomorska and Sophie Vanhoonacker, "The Emerging EU Diplomatic System: Opportunities and Challenges after 'Lisbon'", *The Hague Journal of Diplomacy* 7, no. 1 (January 2012): 1–9.

10 See Janne E. Nijman, "Renaissance of the City as Global Actor", in *The Transformation of Foreign Policy*, ed. Gunther Hellmann, Andreas Fahrmeir and Miloš Vec (Oxford: Oxford University Press, 2016), 209–41.

er more frequent 'state' visits to their foreign counterparts."[11] City governments engage in a variety of international activities and receive increasing recognition for this role. The increasing engagement by local governments in peaceful areas or countries to support their counterparts in more troubled regions received special attention at the *First World Conference on City Diplomacy* in The Hague in 2008.[12] City governments have become organized themselves in one general NGO, *United Cities and Local Governments*, which has observer status with the United Nations.

Subnational levels of federal nations constitute a special case. U.S. states ranging from California and Florida to New York and Massachusetts have representations in various foreign capitals, as do Canadian provinces, such as British Columbia, Quebec and Ontario. Scotland, Wales, Catalonia and Bavaria are other examples of regional diplomatic representation. Public diplomacy, treaty-making, transnational partnerships and participation in multilateral organizations and networks are examples of diplomatic activity by federated entities.[13]

While the diplomatic representation of subnational actors is still relatively marginal, it is not farfetched to anticipate that their role will be enhanced in 21st century diplomacy, considering their critical role in the global economy.

Transnational representation

Given their enhanced role, transnational actors (TNAs) of various kinds – NGOs or civil society organizations, advocacy networks, party associations, philanthropic foundations, multinational corporations – have begun to claim, and are increasingly granted, representation in various diplomatic forums. For instance, some 3,000 NGOs now have consultative status with the Economic and Social Council of the United Nations (ECOSOC), as

---

11 Geoffrey Allen Pigman, *Contemporary Diplomacy* (Cambridge: Polity Press, 2010), 47.

12 Alexandra Sizoo and Arne Musch, "City Diplomacy: The Role of Local Governments in Conflict Prevention, Peace-Building and Post-Conflict Reconstruction", in *City Diplomacy*, ed. Arne Musch, Chris van der Valk, Alexandra Sizoo and Kian Tajbakhsh (The Hague: VNG International, 2008), 7–25 (7), http://bibalex.org/baifa/Attachment/Documents/480503.pdf (accessed 25 March 2018).

13 See David Criekemans, "Regional Sub-State Diplomacy from a Comparative Perspective: Quebec, Scotland, Bavaria, Catalonia, Wallonia and Flanders", *The Hague Journal of Diplomacy* 5, no. 1 (January 2010): 37–64; Pigman, *Contemporary Diplomacy* (see note 11), 47.

compared to 41 in 1948. The openness toward NGOs has subsequently spread to other parts of the UN system, generating a pattern where few or no UN bodies remain entirely closed to TNAs.[14]

States and international institutions are engaging TNAs as policy experts, service providers, compliance watchdogs, and stakeholder representatives. A dataset, containing information on formal TNA access to 298 organizational bodies of 50 international organizations during the time period 1950–2010, shows that, while hardly any of these organizations were open in 1950, more than 75 percent provide access in 2010.[15]

In addition to gaining access to diplomatic forums, TNAs can enact diplomatic roles by means of informal networking. Prominent examples of networking between states, NGOs and international organizations include the processes leading to the Ottawa Treaty in 1997 banning landmines and the creation of the International Criminal Court in 2002. In global health governance the Bill & Melinda Gates Foundation has emerged as a major player. Actors behind popular digital platforms, such as Google and Facebook, have a considerable political impact by how they organize our access to information. While they have not become actively involved in diplomatic processes thus far, their central position in today's world will inevitably draw them into the diplomatic realm before the end of the century. However, in a passive way, these platforms already impact the way diplomacy is conducted as well as the international standing of diplomats.

In sum, one may speak of a transnational turn in diplomacy. Senior diplomats admit that traditional bilateral and multilateral diplomacy has been "progressively supplemented by transnational issues which may or may not involve government-to-government activity."[16] However, TNA representation is problematic. Whereas TNAs typically claim to represent a 'global civil society,' a disproportionate number of them are based in North America or Europe. "As of 2007, 66 per cent of the then 3,050 NGOs with consultative status at the ECOSOC came from North America or Euro-

14 See Jonas Tallberg and Christer Jönsson, "Transnational Actor Participation in International Institutions: Where, Why, and with What Consequences?", in *Transnational Actors in Global Governance*, ed. Christer Jönsson and Jonas Tallberg (Basingstoke: Palgrave Macmillan, 2010), 1–21.

15 See Jonas Tallberg, Thomas Sommerer, Theresa Squatrito and Christer Jönsson, *The Opening Up of International Organizations: Transnational Access in Global Governance* (Basingstoke: Palgrave Macmillan, 2010).

16 Keith Hamilton and Richard Langhorne, *The Practice of Diplomacy: Its Evolution, Theory and Administration*, 2nd ed. (London and New York: Routledge, 2011), 267.

pe."[17] This imbalance seriously reduces the legitimacy of their claims to represent the underprivileged and give voice to the voiceless. The crucial question is whether TNAs from the poor half of the world will acquire the necessary resources to be represented in international forums in the 21st century.

Conclusion

Representation is not a simple and static concept, but a complex and dynamic one. Changes in the parameters of diplomatic representation in the 21st century warrant reflection among practitioners and students alike. In this chapter, I have pointed to some, but by no means all, contemporary issues of representation. I have raised questions, but have not provided any answers. My point is that subtle shifts in the non-technological foundations of diplomacy need to be noted along with the more dramatic changes in information technology when discussing the evolution of diplomacy in the 21st century.

As symbolic representatives of states, diplomatic agents face challenges in terms of increased vulnerability and demands for reflecting multiethnic societies. The problems of acting for others, discussed here, pertain to the changing nature of principals: the difference between democratic and authoritarian states; and the specific complications associated with divided states and populist regimes.

As for non-state representation, the uncertain future development of the EU will determine the significance of the supranational challenge, with no rival regional diplomatic actors in sight. Subnational representation will, in all likelihood, remain of marginal importance, unless states abandon their diplomatic role. For example, the United States' withdrawal from the Paris Agreement triggered individual U.S. states to become more active in the international climate regime. The transnational challenge, on the other hand, has transformative potential by eroding the exclusive cross-border authority of states.

Representation, in sum, is best understood as a *process* rather than a static relationship. It is a process of mutual interaction between principals and agents.[18] Some authors have suggested that the notion of "plastic control",

17 Charlotte Dany, *Global Governance and NGO Participation: Shaping the Information Society in the United Nations* (London and New York: Routledge, 2013), 8.
18 Sobolewski, "Electors and Representatives" (see note 3), 106–07.

introduced by Karl Popper to describe the relation between two interacting and indeterminate systems, may help us to understand this mutual relationship, at the same time as it points to the difficulties in defining representation in more precise terms.[19]

19 J. Roland Pennock and John W. Chapman, "Preface", in *Representation*, ed. Pennock and Chapman (see note 3), xiii–xv (xiv).

Trends and Counter-Trends in Digital Diplomacy*

Corneliu Bjola

The most fascinating aspect of technological disruption is its remarkable capacity for both destruction and creation. By marginalising or even eliminating ways in which people do their work in a specific field of activity, new technologies create pervasive conditions for active and enduring resistance against them. On the other hand, by laying the groundwork for new economic or social opportunities, they also stimulate new thinking and innovative practices that reinforce and sustain these technologies in the long term. The ability of disruptive technologies to entrench themselves in society depends, therefore, on how the balance between the trends and counter-trends that they abruptly unleash is ultimately decided. This observation may prove particularly valuable for understanding the evolution of digital diplomacy and the extent to which the recent adoption of digital technologies by Ministries of Foreign Affairs (MFAs) will be able to substantially change the way in which diplomacy is practiced, or whether it will have only a marginal effect on its mode of operation.

Two opposing mega-trends are particularly important to consider when examining the transformative potential of digital technologies on diplomatic relations. The *first mega-trend* actively encourages digital adoption and is driven by the dual process of rapid acceleration of technological disruption, on the one hand, and the MFAs commitment to thrive in an increasingly competitive environment, on the other hand. While it took the telephone 75 years to reach 100 million users worldwide, the mobile phone and its most popular app, Facebook, needed only 16 and 4 ½ years respectively to pass this milestone.[1] Technological acceleration thus puts significant pressure on MFAs to develop strong capacities for understanding the potential of digital technologies in their activity and for devising

---

* A Spanish translation of this chapter was published as "Diplomacia digital 2.0: tendencias y resistencias" in *Revista Mexicana de Política Exterior*, no. 113 (May–August 2018): 35–52.

1 Ralf Dreischmeier, Karalee Close and Philippe Trichet, "The Digital Imperative" (The Boston Consulting Group, 2 March 2015), https://www.bcgperspectives.com/content/articles/digital_economy_technology_strategy_digital_imperative/ (accessed 18 July 2018).

strategies for mainstreaming and tailoring them to short and long-term foreign policy objectives. The failure to do so, risks exposing MFAs to the problem of not being able to maintain their ability to meaningfully influence policy outcomes in the international arena. Three areas should be analysed closer by MFAs as the rate of technological disruption accelerates: the context, the process, and the structure of the digital diplomatic transformation.

What's the difference between AR, VR, and MR?
Augmented reality (AR) adds digital elements to a live view often by using the camera on a smartphone. Examples of augmented reality experiences include Snapchat lenses and the game Pokemon Go. Virtual reality (VR) implies a complete immersion experience that shuts out the physical world. Using VR devices such as HTC Vive, Oculus Rift or Google Cardboard, users can be transported into a number of real-world and imagined environments such as the middle of a squawking penguin colony or even the back of a dragon.
In a mixed reality (MR) experience, which combines elements of both AR and VR, real-world and digital objects interact. Mixed reality technology is just now starting to take off with Microsoft's HoloLens being one of the most notable early mixed reality apparatuses.
Source: see https://www.fi.edu/difference-between-ar-vr-and-mr

Context: From Institutional-based to Ecosystem Approaches

From an institutional perspective, the MFA's organisational culture constitutes a critical interface for digital adaptation and can make a big difference as to whether diplomats would perceive digital technologies as a threat or as an opportunity in their work.[2] However, as the success or failure of technological innovations is also dependent on the quality of the broader ecosystem that supports them, MFAs would also need a better understanding of the technological context in which they operate in order to figure out which digital trends to follow and which not. The 3G mobile

2 Corneliu Bjola, *Adapting Diplomacy to the Digital Age: Managing the Organisational Culture of Ministries of Foreign Affairs*, Working Paper, Project "Diplomacy in the 21st Century" (Berlin Stiftung Wissenschaft und Politik, March 2017), https://www.swp-berlin.org/fileadmin/contents/products/arbeitspapiere/WP_Diplomacy21_No9_Corneliu_Bjola_01.pdf (accessed 22 June 2017).

technology made possible, for instance, the development and spread of social media networks. The 5G technology, which is due to arrive in just a few years, will likely usher in a whole new level of technological disruption, which could lead to the mass adoption of an entire range of tech tools of growing relevance for diplomacy, such as virtual reality (VR) and augmented reality (AR) in public diplomacy or artificial intelligence in consular services.

In fact, as Sandre points out, the future is already here.[3] For example, in May 2016, the Italian Ministry of Foreign Affairs and International Cooperation announced that it had joined the Google Art Project – an online technology platform developed by Google to promote and protect culture – to open its art collection and virtually display 176 works of art.[4] In July 2016, NATO's Euro-Atlantic Disaster Response Coordination Centre (EADRCC) and Romania, with support from the Joint Health Agriculture and Food Group (JHAFG) and the Civil Protection Group (CPG), partnered to organize a disaster response exercise using VR to simulate a large-scale emergency situation with multiple casualties and the evacuation of a large number of people.[5] AR has been somewhat slower than VR to catch on with the public, but the technology is advancing fast[6] and should be able to generate a steady flow of apps, including for diplomacy, relatively quickly.

Immersive AR systems could prove useful, for instance, for creating highly interactive public diplomacy campaigns or for tailoring consular services to individual needs, possibly in combination with iBeacon technology.[7] Artificial intelligence (AI) is also making steady progress in con-

---

3 Andreas Sandre, "2016 in Review: Virtual Reality for Digital Diplomacy", Digital Diplomacy, 2016, https://medium.com/digital-diplomacy/2016-in-review-virtual-reality-for-digital-diplomacy-b461ac2ff16 (accessed 4 September 2017).

4 Italian Ministry of Foreign Affairs, "Collezione Farnesina", 2016, https://artsandculture.google.com/partner/ministero-affari-esteri (accessed 4 September 2017).

5 "Romania Hosts NATO Exercise in a Virtual World" (NATO, 2016), https://www.youtube.com/watch?v=dZ3S4OpKlFs& feature=youtu.be (accessed 3 September 2017).

6 Tim Perdue, "Applications of Augmented Reality", *Lifewire* (updated 20 June 2018), https://www.lifewire.com/applications-of-augmented-reality-2495561 (accessed 18 July 2018).

7 Beacons are buttons or links to the physical world: in the same way that web pages rely on buttons as a primary way for user interaction, beacons are used by apps to trigger events and call actions, allowing users to interact with digital or physical things, such as door locks, discounts, automation systems or simple notifications. See details at "What Is iBeacon?" (Beecon, 2016), http://www.beaconsandwich.com/what-is-ibeacon.html (accessed 1 September 2017).

sular affairs. At the lower end of the complexity scale, chat-bots now assist with visa applications, legal aid for refugees, and consular registrations.[8] More sophisticated algorithms are being developed by MFAs to either advance the spread of positive narratives or inhibit online disinformation and propaganda.[9] In sum, the second wave of technological disruption is already under way, but its success will greatly depend on the reliability of the ecosystem in which embassies operate: superfast broadband availability, clear strategic vision, strong demand for digital services, cost effectiveness, and skilled personnel.

Process: From Re-action to Pro-action

Staying ahead of the technological curve will likely require a cognitive shift from following to anticipating and possibly pushing new trends. By reacting to the rise of social media, MFAs have managed, for instance, to leverage the power of these tools for maximising their role in public diplomacy, crisis communication and diaspora engagement. However, by anticipating new trends, they could better operate in an increasingly competitive digital environment and set the rules and standards of digital practice before others have the chance to do it. Pushing new trends could also prove highly beneficial, as the 'first mover' advantage could help digital pioneers to secure extra recognition and influence, thus boosting their 'soft power' credentials as diplomatic leaders and innovators.

'Going pro-active' could happen horizontally, when successful digital practices are extended from one diplomatic area to another (e.g., by transferring techniques of digital listening and engagement used in public diplomacy to crisis communication) or vertically, when the input/output value of digital technologies is maximised (e.g., by making better use of

8 "Immigration Attorney 2.0" (Visabot, 2016), https://visabot.co/ (accessed 1 June 2017); Elena Cresci, "Chatbot That Overturned 160,000 Parking Fines Now Helping Refugees Claim Asylum", *The Guardian*, 6 March 2017, https://www.theguardian.com/technology/2017/mar/06/chatbot-donotpay-refugees-claim-asylum-legal-aid (accessed 7 September 2017); "Most Singaporeans Do Not E-register before Travelling", *Channel New Asia*, 3 March 2017, http://www.channelnewsasia.com/news/singapore/most-singaporeans-do-not-e-register-before-travelling-mfa-8775352 (accessed 6 September 2017).

9 Simon Cocking, "Using Algorithms to Achieve Digital Diplomacy", *Irish Tech News*, 19 September 2016, http://irishtechnews.ie/using-algorithms-to-achieve-digital-diplomacy-a-conversation-with-elad-ratson-director-of-rd-at-ministry-of-foreign-affairs/ (accessed 8 September 2017).

big data via predictive analysis and algorithms). For example, by mining open-source data from social media, satellite imagery and blogs, the Embers project sponsored by the Intelligence Advanced Research Projects Activity (IARPA) has generated, since 2012, highly accurate forecasts of influenza-like illness case counts, rare disease outbreaks, civil unrest, domestic political crises, and elections.[10] Big data analytics could thus become an indispensable tool for embassies for getting a comprehensive, in-depth and reliable understanding of the local conditions in which they operate in real-time, which in turn could help them better tailor and fine-tune their bilateral diplomatic approach.

Structure: From Centralisation to 'Network of Networks'

A dense digital environment, with a high rate of technological innovation, favours and rewards creativity and experimentation over hierarchy and procedures. This means that in order to adapt more effectively to technological challenges, MFAs would need to relax the constraints of institutional centralisation and instead encourage forms and modes of digital interaction tailored to the specific profile of its constitutive diplomatic networks. As noted by the authors of the *Future of Diplomacy Report*, the nature of the national diplomatic environment is changing from one that privileges the role of the MFAs to one which places it within a broader construct – that of the national diplomatic system (NDS), which covers the complex network of governmental and non-governmental institutions that inform and shape a country's international policy objectives.[11] Building on this insight, one could argue that MFAs' digital architecture could be best captured by the concept of a digital diplomatic system (DDS), which refers to the 'network of networks' of embassies, consulates, think tanks, private companies, international organisations and civil society groups that contribute and shape the digital diplomatic profile of a country.

DDS consists of three key layers. The *first layer* is demand driven and connects institutional actors, groups and stakeholders that directly benefit from digital diplomatic programs. It may include diaspora groups in need

---

10 "Embers" (Discovery Analytics Center at Virginia Tech, 2016), http://dac.cs.vt.edu/research-project/embers/ (accessed 9 September 2017).

11 Brian Hocking, Jan Melissen, Shaun Riordan and Paul Sharp, *Futures for Diplomacy: Integrative Diplomacy for the 21st Century* (The Hague: Netherlands Institute of International Relations 'Clingendael', 2012), 53, https://www.clingendael.org/sites/default/files/pdfs/20121030_research_melissen.pdf (accessed 3 May 2018).

of good digital consular services, embassies in critical spots facing public diplomacy challenges, and think tanks providing consultancy to MFAs on digital matters. The *second layer* is functional and task-oriented. Diplomatic missions to international organisations would benefit, for instance, from close collaborative efforts aimed at exploring and testing the potential of digital technologies in multilateral contexts. Similarly, embassies and consulates based in conflict-risk regions could share experiences and best practices regarding the use of digital technologies in crisis situations. The *third layer* is tech-oriented and practice-oriented and seeks to advance digital innovation and dissemination of good practices of digital diplomacy. Digital pioneers working in embassies, academics researching digital diplomatic practices and private IT companies are the most likely nodes in this network. The three DDS layers have flexible configurations and they may occasionally intersect or clash, but they can offer MFAs a much-needed boost of forward-thinking creativity and ambition to their digital diplomacy objectives and strategies, in a manner that does not require a fundamental rewriting of their institutional structure.

The *second mega-trend* works in a different direction by building resistance against the use of digital technologies. Unlike the case above, where MFAs are concerned about the risk of missing out on potential opportunities created by technological breakthroughs, this counter-driver raises questions about whether the costs of 'going digital' may not actually exceed its benefits. Paradoxically, the success of digitization may plant the seeds for the rise of a powerful counter-trend to MFAs' efforts to further integrate and institutionalise digital technologies in their work. Emotional contagion, algorithmic determinism and strategic entropy are three ways in which this counter-trend is more likely to manifest itself.

Post-truth: From Fact-based Reasoning to Emotional Commodification

Diplomatic engagement requires a minimum level of shared understanding and mutual openness in order to work. Such possibility arguably dissipates when emotions overwhelmingly frame and dominate the discourse by which opinions are formed online, and when facts are pushed into a secondary or marginal position. Emotional commodification (i.e., deliberate amplification of emotional content in the online discourse) has become a regular pattern of engagement on social media platforms as it helps digital influencers control the scope and direction of the online conversation. Posts connected with high-arousal emotions, whether positive or negative, have greater viral potential than those containing low-arousal emotions.[12] At the same time, emotional valence (i.e., the degree of positivity or negativity of an emotion) can trigger, by over-exposure, desired reactions from the audience.[13] Emotional commodification has negative implications for digital diplomacy for two reasons. First, it enables the formation of echo-chambers, whereby MFAs and embassies end up "preaching to the choir" of sympathetic online followers, thus failing to reach constituencies outside the self-reinforcing "digital bubble" of like-minded followers.[14] Second, it favours a 'post-truth' environment in which 'fake news' and disinformation thrive, thus making more difficult for digital diplomats to articulate their message and engage with their audience or to defend themselves against defamatory claims.

As the connection between emotions and social media becomes stronger and more sophisticated, the question of how digital diplomats can adapt to an emotionally charged form of social communication can no longer be ignored. The concept of digital emotional intelligence (DEI) might offer a solution. First developed by Salovey and Sluyter, DEI covers four distinct dimensions, namely, the ability:

1. To perceive or experience emotions accurately,
2. To use emotional information to facilitate thought and action,
3. To understand the meaning and significance of emotions, and
4. To manage emotions in one's self and others.[15]

DEI cannot prevent the formation of echo-chambers or the dissemination of digital propaganda, but it can help social media users to better cope with them. For example, DEI can help digital users better discriminate between genuine vs. false emotional expressions, facilitate a better understanding of how emotions affect their thinking, enable them to recognise the sources and implications of their emotions, and regulate their level of detachment or engagement to an emotional trigger in a particular situa-

---

12 Neil Davidson, "What Are the Key Emotional Triggers for Online Video?" (MWP Digital Media, 4 December 2013), https://mwpdigitalmedia.com/blog/key-emotional-triggers-online-video/ (accessed 18 July 2018).

13 Emilio Ferrara and Zeyao Yang, "Measuring Emotional Contagion in Social Media", *PLOS ONE* 10, no. 11 (November 2015), http://journals.plos.org/plosone/article?id=10.1371/journal.pone.0142390 (accessed 18 July 2018).

14 Corneliu Bjola, "Digital Diplomacy and the Bubble Effect: The NATO Scenario" (Los Angeles: USC Center on Public Diplomacy, 8 March 2016), http://uscpublicdiplomacy.org/blog/digital-diplomacy-and-bubble-effect-nato-scenario (accessed 17 June 2017).

15 Peter Salovey and David J. Sluyter, *Emotional Development and Emotional Intelligence: Educational Implications* (New York: Basic Books, 1997).

tion. Paying close attention to how genuinely and intensely people feel about a particular situation in their online communication can help avoid embarrassing moments with potentially disruptive implications for bilateral relations. In short, DEI could facilitate careful digital navigation through emotion-laden situations and steer the conversation back on a path informed by fact-based reasoning. MFAs and governments should therefore invest in the education of their staff to be better equipped to navigate this digital environment.

Automation: From Relationship-building to Robo-trolling

MFAs' interest in digital technologies primarily lies with their capacities to reach out to online influencers and develop multiple networks of engagement with and across a variety of constituencies. By 'going digital', the once secretive and exclusive domain of the elite has also gone public, requiring diplomats to regularly look outside their once closed doors, and perhaps more importantly, for the first time, allowing citizens to look in.[16] Being able to reach out to millions of people, directly and in real-time thus represents a remarkable opportunity for MFAs to redefine themselves in the Digital Age, including by building strong relationships with foreign publics. This ability could nevertheless be severely tested and even compromised by the growing use of algorithms as instruments of conversation monitoring, agenda setting and message dissemination. Recent studies have shown that up to 15 percent of Twitter accounts are in fact bots rather than people, and this number is bound to increase in the future.[17] One could safely argue that whenever AI entities overtake humans in the population of digital users, the possibility of MFAs and embassies to develop meaningful relationships with online publics drastically decreases.

Furthermore, it is not only the presence of algorithms that may hinder digital diplomatic interactions, but also the purpose for which they are used. Intriguingly, the 'dark side' of digital technologies (e.g., disinformation, propaganda and infowar tactics) has proved to be the most fertile ground for the proliferation of bots. A recent report produced by the NATO's Strategic Center of Excellence in Latvia has found, for instance, that

16 Corneliu Bjola and Jennifer Cassidy, "Gone Digital: Digital Diplomacy at the University of Oxford", *Border Crossing* 1, no. 2 (2015): 10–12 (10).

17 Michael Newberg, "As Many as 48 Million Twitter Accounts Aren't People, Says Study", *CNBC*, 10 March 2017, https://www.cnbc.com/2017/03/10/nearly-48-million-twitter-accounts-could-be-bots-says-study.html (accessed 12 September 2017).

the 'Twitter conversation' about NATO-related news is mainly bots talking to other bots, bots promoting third-party content and bots incrementally building more believable profiles.[18] Some also fear that AI could soon make it easier for adversaries to divide and dishearten alliances, for example, by undermining trust among countries fighting on the same side and by discrediting their intelligence.[19] While these developments have a predominant intelligence and military profile, they nevertheless have important diplomatic repercussions, as their use is mainly tailored to tearing down political institutions and diplomatic relationships, not building them up.

Robo-trolling (i.e., use of algorithms for content promotion and/or disruption) is now part of the digital landscape and without new rules by which the anonymity of social media users can be removed, it is likely to remain so. Digital diplomats may not be therefore able to prevent AI from disrupting their relationship building activities, but they may contain some of its negative ramifications. The "Three A's" (activity, anonymity, and amplification) – techniques of bot and botnet discovery and identification[20] – should, for instance, be widely disseminated through the digital diplomatic system to increase awareness and resistance against possible sources of manipulation. At the same time, MFAs may deploy AI tools themselves, such as Google's Perspective as a way of reducing the pressure on their limited resources for mapping and filtering abusive comments that disrupt their online conversation.[21] In more serious situations, when the robo-trolling crosses the threshold of disinformation into aggressive propaganda and infowar, more sophisticated measures of digital containment would need to be considered. The goals would be supporting media literacy and source criticism, encouraging institutional resilience, and pro-

18 Donald N. Jensen and Michal Harmata, "What to Expect when You're Expecting Bots?" (Washington, D.C.: Center for European Policy Analysis, 2017), http://infowar.cepa.org/EN/what-to-expect-when-youre-expecting-bots (accessed 9 September 2017).

19 Tomáš Valášek, "How Artificial Intelligence Could Disrupt Alliances" (Carnegie Europe, 31 August 2017), https://medium.com/@Carnegie_Europe/how-artificial-intelligence-could-disrupt-alliances-9fdb98b4c11d (accessed 18 July 2018).

20 Ben Nimmo, "#BotSpot: Twelve Ways to Spot a Bot" (Atlantic Council's Digital Forensic Research Lab, 2017), https://medium.com/dfrlab/botspot-twelve-ways-to-spot-a-bot-aedc7d9c110c (accessed 11 September 2017).

21 Jigsaw, "Perspective", 2017, https://www.perspectiveapi. com (accessed 11 September 2017); Murgia Madhumita, "Google Launches Robo-tool to Flag Hate Speech Online", *Financial Times*, 23 February 2017, https://www.ft.com/content/8786cce8-f91e-11e6-bd4e-68d53499ed71 (accessed 11 September 2017).

moting a clear and coherent strategic narrative capable of containing the threat from inconsistent counter-messaging.[22]

Strategic Entropy: From Digital Outputs to Policy Outcomes

It is also important to remind ourselves that digital diplomacy is not supposed to be an end in itself, but rather to inform and serve foreign policy objectives. The disruptive character of technological breakthroughs may lead, however, at least in the initial stage, to a decoupling of digital diplomacy from foreign policy. Quick adoption of digital tools without an overarching strategy of how they should be used in support of certain foreign policy objectives is likely to create problems of policy coordination and implementation. Digital enthusiasts working in embassies may seek to push ahead with experimentation and innovation, especially in public diplomacy, and with varying degrees of success. At the same time, MFA 'mandarins' facing budgetary and bureaucratic pressures to demonstrate 'value for money' may seek to slow down the process of digital adoption and to align it to the pace of foreign policy making. The risk for MFAs entailed by the 'tug of war' between digital enthusiasts and sceptics is to find themselves either running underfunded digital campaigns with no clear direction or strategic compass, or uncritically embracing rigid 'diplometric' models, predominantly quantitative, for designing and assessing the success of digital activities. In both cases, the result is likely to be the same: a middle-ground approach that would neither promote innovative digital outputs as favoured by enthusiasts nor reliably inform foreign policy outcomes as advocated by sceptics.

One way in which this tension could be mitigated is by drawing on the output vs. outcome distinction in public policy analysis so as to separate means (what digital diplomacy does) from results (what digital diplomacy accomplishes).[23] Outputs reflect on-going consequences of digital activities, while outcomes cover broader influences of the digital outputs on policy objectives. As argued elsewhere, it makes sense to prioritise the impact of digital outputs at the expense of policy outcomes, when digital activities involve complex operations, large audiences, and lengthy periods of imple-

22 Corneliu Bjola and James Pamment, "Digital Containment: Revisiting Containment Strategy in the Digital Age", *Global Affairs* 2, no. 2 (2016): 131–42.

23 Peter Knoepfel, Corinne Larrue, Michael Hill and Frédéric Varone, *Public Policy Analysis* (Bristol: Bristol University Press, 2011), 11.

mentation, as it may often happen in digital public diplomacy.[24] In such cases, if quantitatively strong outputs (content, reach, engagement) are generated in a consistent fashion, then one would expect positive policy outcomes (e.g., perception changes in the target audience) to follow as well at some point. On the other hand, digital engagements are more conducive to informing outcome-based strategies, when they involve conventional operations, with small or medium-size audiences, requiring short periods of implementation. Consular crisis communication is particularly amenable to this approach since the goal of assisting nationals in times of terrorist attacks or natural disasters with timely and accurate information (output) about how to protect themselves from harm during crises (outcome) is a relatively straightforward strategy in which digital outputs are informed by and assessed against tangible policy goals. In sum, managing strategic entropy is a matter of understanding how to prioritise and balance digital outputs vs. policy outcomes.

To conclude, the future of digital diplomacy lies within the ability of MFAs to exploit the opportunities generated by technological disruption, while guarding itself against the potential pitfalls that its early success might create. If technological acceleration will be seen as an opportunity for ecosystem-based, pro-active, and network-oriented adaptation, then digital diplomacy is likely to penetrate the deep core of the diplomatic DNA. If, on the other hand, digitization fails to restrain emotional contagion, algorithmic determinism and strategic entropy, then MFAs will likely slow down their efforts to integrate digital technologies in their work.

---

24 Corneliu Bjola, "Getting Digital Diplomacy Right: What Quantum Theory Can Teach Us about Measuring Impact", *Global Affairs* 2, no. 3 (2016): 345–53.

Critical Digital Diplomacy and How Theory Can Inform Practice*

Emillie V. de Keulenaar and Jan Melissen

A debate on the impact of digitization on diplomatic practice is currently taking place in most of the world's diplomatic services. This debate serves as a reminder of how important it is to continue discerning the political significance of digital technologies in diplomacy and to confront the emerging reality of diplomatic engagement in a digitized world, rather than focusing exclusively on applying digital tools to existing practices. In 2016 and 2017, illicit electronic intervention in democratic elections and referenda in Europe and the United States has turned the issue of digital diplomacy's 'weaponization' into headline news. In just a couple of years the dominant tone in the narrative on digital diplomacy has transformed from one of optimism about social media's mobilization potential and a boost for democratization, to one of gloominess about 'fake news' and the stealthy intrusion in social media conversations by bots and trolls controlled from authoritarian countries. U.S.-based tech giants are accused of ethically questionable trade in personal data harvested from social networking sites, whilst the influence operations of the UK-based company Cambridge Analytica have caused alarm about the commercial behaviour of web developers in the social and political realm. More than five years after the social media optimism associated with the Arab Spring, some ministries of foreign affairs (MFAs) that wanted to be seen as early social media adopters may wonder whether they have rushed into the social media domain without sufficient critical reflection.

Rather than joining current affairs commentary on the impact of social media in international politics, we will, in this chapter, first turn to literature that can help throw a light on underlying issues. We take a close look at new media studies to add to our understanding of the role of digital technologies as media and infrastructures to current diplomatic processes. It is our aim to inform the study of diplomacy as well as diplomatic prac-

* This essay builds on our discussion in a previously published article: Jan Melissen and Emillie de Keulenaar, "Critical Digital Diplomacy as a Global Challenge: The South Korean Experience", *Global Policy* 8, no. 3 (September 2017): 294–302.

tice with relevant theoretical insights and conceptualizations from this field. We conclude with general policy recommendations for MFAs.

Technology and Diplomatic Practice

Agreement on essential terminology and a shared understanding of core concepts matters – and is not just relevant for academics. Reminiscent of references to 'soft power' in the past 25 years, by politicians and diplomats as much as scholars, basic terminology in the digital diplomacy debate is used rather loosely. In this context of changing practices, we need to reflect on the depth and extent of digital technology, first as a new medium for states and other international actors to communicate and conduct relations, and secondly as a condition. The digital age is increasingly permeating the way in which new generations experience their life and work.

Before arriving at conclusions about the impact of technological change in the practice of international relations, it is worthwhile to continue reflecting on the capacities of these new technologies. It is safe to suggest that many MFAs' initiatives aimed at encouraging the use of social media have been insufficiently grounded in an analysis of digital technologies in terms of what they bring to modern literacy and to the conditions in which diplomacy is now practiced. Comprising these conditions are the underlying techniques that constitute digital technologies, whether they are referred to generally as algorithms or to other types of computational systems, including search engines, recommenders or newsfeeds. Benefitting from the mediatory capacity of digitization and datafication practices, these techniques have become ubiquitous access points to culture, politics and economic activities. Designing these and other pieces of software grants tech actors a powerful political impact in how they formalize, organize and repurpose information and cultural capital today.

This invites the field of digital diplomacy to interrogate how digital technologies go about redesigning one's access to processes relevant to diplomacy. Just as Facebook may have altered one's access to social life, political action and the marketplace of ideas, other tech actors and their platforms have leverage in redesigning several processes that constitute international relations. The potential of new technologies to assist knowledge management combined with the potential of big data concerning intricate issue areas and for the purposes of forecasting, are bound to have a great impact on diplomacy's chief function: international negotiation. Human decisions will remain as important as ever and data do not speak; but acting upon how data and the ideas they constitute are organized by important algorithmic systems and platform affordances may add to 'the art of negotiation' and involve a great deal of complexity management.

In this sense, we see in the broader realm of cultural relations how digital culture impacts on transnational exchange and conditions for the creation of new ideas in ways that interplay with international and domestic public consensus. New warfare tactics used by Russian military intelligence during the U.S. 2016 presidential elections have in fact directly tapped into this question by interplaying with popularity and attention metrics as they distributed sensational, 'fake' news to feed into partisan divide on Facebook, Twitter and YouTube. The influence of digital platforms in the fields of culture and social relations may equally mean that they are of greater relevance to increasingly 'societized' diplomatic practices, ones that include diverse stakeholders and address a variety of non-traditional issues on the international agenda. Concretely, such societized diplomacy results in new dynamics in government-society relations and, arguably, more domestically oriented MFAs.

Many international challenges of our time have acquired some kind of digital dimension, such that their corresponding technologies provide a platform for social, political and economic activities that could be understood as being computationally formalized. It is one thing to assess Facebook as a vector of diplomatic messages. Another aspect would be to assess the self-same politics partly as products of the platform mechanisms that process and organize them as data – or indeed to assess platform mechanisms and other algorithms as political processes in their own right. Doing so may invite diplomats to locate various issues relevant to foreign policy within their respective technical context. For example, to what extent do information filtering systems such as YouTube's recommender follow EU guidelines to distribute and 'recommend' videos in a pluralistic and diverse fashion? Possible answers to this question touch directly upon how the systematic organization of information through algorithms constitutes the means through which political solutions may be applied. Facebook and Google have already been attempting to tackle problems such as filter bubbles and fake news from a technical standpoint – yet, they may greatly benefit from the perspective of those specialized in interpreting and resolving the nature of such issues, such as conflict and misinformation. Diplomats are in a unique place not just to offer their expertise, but also to formulate their own political philosophy of computational foreign policy by moulding values, strategies and processes proper to their field into information and information-organizing systems.

Such initiatives may come across as naïve for expecting too much of companies driven by private gains and peculiar platform business models.

But it is this very problem that pushes public policy makers to balance the public responsibility of tech actors and their patented systems, both widely originating from the United States, precisely by inviting the actors that design them to share a continuous, collaborative responsibility with foreign, public counterparts. This collaborative responsibility would be facilitated by diplomats attuned to the technical and political dimensions of the issues that such systems reproduce.

Digital Literacy and Awareness in Diplomacy

As mentioned above, pessimism and the extent to which misuse of social media complicates international relationships seem to have become dominant in recent debates about digital diplomacy. We maintain nevertheless that, because they provide one with additional capacities to put ideas and policy into (technical) practice, digital technologies should above all be recognized as a source of creativity for diplomats. Their relevance comes above all from their capacities as media, and, in this sense, as grounds for new literacies. They can be more than simply using available devices and services such as email, Twitter or Facebook. Digital technologies can be compared to writing and speech in that they allow users or 'writers' to collect, organize and repurpose information on various aspects of reality, whether it be data about or from individual users, objects, institutions, or from more complex processes. Digital literacy would then range from engaging with ready-made software as a user all the way to coding it, gaining leverage over how users shall access it and what it allows one to do with it.

The so-called 'digital divide' may then not be just one between populations that have or lack the means to access these technologies, but also one between more or less 'digitally literate' citizens and governance. Big powers, small non-governmental organizations (NGOs) and diplomatic actors of any kind could employ programming languages as tools to operationalize data by way of realizing certain interests and objectives in the form of usable software for public usage or techniques designed for internal purposes, whether they be for reference (for example, with data analysis), communication or other programmable purposes. In the same way that certain companies conceive of sociality, transportation or marketing in terms of information and information systems, digital diplomacy would invite policy to conceive of entities, processes, strategies and values relevant to diplomacy at least partly as computational entities. Digital literacy would then also refer to the ability to take on computation as a form of governance attuned to contemporary instruments of power, such as software. Adopting these means to digital literacy is what allows an institution such as diplomacy to exercise active decision-making with technical actors and towards the programs and data that touch upon their craft.

Thus, digital literacy would equally amount to the individual ability to make an informed assessment of how these technologies are designed, and in what terms diplomats can approach those that design them: tech actors. The value of approaching them lies in gaining access to information about how their systems work, what they do with data tied to issues at stake for MFAs, and in negotiating ways to alter their systems, the collection and curation of platform-owned data in ways favourable to all actors affected by those issues. One of the challenges, here, would lie in conceiving of ways to mediate the interests of tech actors, whose primary goal is to think in terms of product design, and public actors, who would in most cases advance the causes of several normative questions. Ultimately, combining essentially technical and political rationales is what the deliberative process of digital diplomats could come down to. Part of this process entails proposing how tech actors could formalize the normative values that drive the agenda of diplomacy as computational values – an exercise that may well invite diplomats and their tech actors into a joint deliberation.

MFAs have therefore started thinking about the fundamental implications of digital transformation for the physical structures of their headquarters and embassies. Following the private sector and other government departments, they are currently enhancing their capacity to take advantage of big data analysis in the interests of foreign policy-making. A challenge for foreign policy bureaucracies steeped in centuries of diplomatic tradition is that they lack the intuitive, post-disciplinary, 'native' character of some NGOs and companies that are thriving with the investment and management of data. What may lie further ahead is that MFAs re-conceptualize diplomacy as the management of complexity as much as the management of international relations.

The Softwarization of Diplomatic Practice

Many practitioners appear to see 'digital diplomacy' almost uniquely as an extension of public diplomacy. Within this restricted understanding of the purposes of digital diplomacy, the decreasing trust in information, the privacy concerns of internet users, and the mobility across platforms of young generations amount to new challenges for MFA communication departments. There is however the need to take a broader look and analyse digital technologies as mediating political processes. Diplomatic engagement with digital technologies and the utilization of software for diplomatic purposes is thus to be based on an understanding of the political significance of technicality. The relationship between individual diplomats and digital technology suggests a different history than the way in which predecessors have adopted the use of the telephone (to call), the typewriter (to write), the telegraph (to send encrypted messages) and the personal computer (to write, store, organize and send information).

To be sure, the advent of social media has shown entirely new dynamics in the relationship between diplomacy and technology. Over the past years, many MFAs have invested a great deal in introducing themselves to the social media phenomenon and have started making use of its potential in more and more areas of foreign policy. Following the Arab Spring, a variety of international crises between 2011 and 2015 were major learning opportunities for governments. In a relatively short time span, social media have become indispensable in the delivery of key MFA functions such as public diplomacy and assistance to nationals abroad.

The way in which digital technologies are currently used is often fundamentally similar to the incorporation of various types of 'machines' in 19th and 20th century diplomatic practice: diplomats use what technology offers and is designed to do. Yet, as previously mentioned, part of understanding the digital dimensions of diplomacy today is to make use of digital technologies as metamedia: media that can be used actively and imaginatively to create yet more media, such as software. They offer ready-to-use products such as computers and other hands-on devices, but they also provide the means to create software that is tailored to internal or proactive diplomatic needs. This seems to be the case with what Uber does for transportation, Airbnb for the hospitality industry, Google for documentation, YouTube for filmmaking, Spotify for music, and Facebook and Twitter for personal relations, political careers and political activism. The influence of these platforms resides partly in their organizing and systematizing of digitized data and the transnational mediation of content, whether it is in the form of culture, ideas, knowledge, relations or capital. Such is the power of the daily bread-and-butter in the 'walled gardens' of Google (using its PageRank algorithm), Twitter (selling algorithms to private-sector clients doing business in personal data with governments), YouTube (the second largest engine on the web) and Facebook (at the centre of the debate about the ethical practices of commercial tech giants and the need to tame the influence of the corporate sector). There is now growing awareness that the mediation capacity of these platforms as controlled informational environments is as relevant to the world of diplomacy as it is to the commercial sector.

One important consequence of these fast-moving developments is that the governance of the digital realm needs to catch up. Although not analysed here, reigning in undesirable practices is a collective responsibility of national governments, digital platforms and end-users, which requires innovative forms of governance.

More than a Search for Attention Online

In terms of the kinds of skills needed by foreign policy actors, there is little doubt that the multifaceted nature of the digitization of diplomatic practice amounts to the largest upskilling exercise in the history of diplomacy. For many future diplomats the most important learning will consist of critical knowledge and the use of software and other technical, but no less political, elements constituting digital technologies. From user-friendly interfaces to codes and algorithms, it is this design that they need to examine, critique, and improve in the interests of enhancing policy capacity.

The technical aspects of everything digital are profoundly political, as debates about foreign interference in the 2016 and 2017 U.S. and European election campaigns and the 2018 public outrage about Cambridge Analytica's practices have made abundantly clear. Much more remains hidden in the expanding realm where diplomacy and intelligence increasingly overlap. Common sense in the digital age therefore dictates that diplomats should remain critical of real-life actors behind software, of their intentions and of how they pursue their aims, and to what effect. Politics happens at the earliest stages of the design of software used in the context of international relationships. In recent years, some western governments have lost their relative innocence. They follow the lead of more astute countries – ranging from Russia to Sudan and Israel to Iran – as well as non-governmental actors working in the interests of a better world, or engaged in violent action and with contested motives, such as terrorist groups or rebel movements.

Digital diplomacy is then not so much an active and continuous search for attention online, as it is in a lot of public diplomacy. The practices of digital communication and outreach to foreign and domestic audiences do in fact seem to have disrupted public diplomacy to an extent that deserves urgent examination. As to critical digital diplomacy: it constitutes diplomatic engagement with how culture, information and relations are systematized in software, such as with the counteracting of algorithms that do not work in one's favour. Mechanisms constituting digital technologies can be actively used as tools to operationalize political and diplomatic interests.

The challenge for MFAs is thus to explore all of this and put it into practice. Individual diplomats are in need of concepts to critique and comprehend technicality as a medium for diplomatic strategy and policy implementation. After all, contemporary diplomacy is already enacted in rapidly changing landscapes where new technological tools impact on the nature of international relationships.

Five Policy Recommendations

1. Diplomats should realize that digital diplomacy constitutes engagement with how culture, information and relations are systematized in software, such as with the counteracting of algorithms that do not work in one's favour.
2. As diplomacy is increasingly enacted in a digital environment, diplomats should be critical of real-life actors behind software, of their intentions and how they pursue their aims, and to what effect.
3. MFAs that have the capability to create software for diplomatic purposes but do not yet do so are at a disadvantage in comparison with more astute counterparts and non-governmental actors.
4. Mechanisms constituting digital technologies can be used as a medium to operationalize political and diplomatic interests.
5. Diplomats may act as mediators between platform actors and all others affected by platform systems and data, honing a capacity to invite a dialogue between technical and normative interests.

Perpetual Change: Remarks on Diplomacy Today in the European Union*

Karsten D. Voigt

The number of organized and institutionalized actors actively participating in the international sector is steadily increasing. Synchronously (although the public was not traditionally concerned with foreign policy) sections of the public interconnect on national and international levels.In addition, new partly-, pseudo- or quasi-governmental actors have come along. I will make six observations, drawing mainly from the German experience. The expansion of the diplomatic sphere predominantly relates to the foreign policy of the European member states. This is not a coincidence, since particularly intense communication is taking place between member states of the European Union (EU). Via this communication, the boundaries between domestic and foreign policy as well as between national, intergovernmental and international politics begin to blur. Thus this communication acts as an agent of continuous change for diplomacy, perhaps more so than elsewhere.

1. *New Forms of Communication*

The way foreign policy is conducted needs to adapt continuously. Situations involving crisis and conflict in particular require intense communication among all involved parties. In such situations, a daily exchange of ideas between the capitals implicated in reaching a solution is the rule rather than the exception. Which capitals will be involved in the communication depends on the relevance of the individual states and their leaders to

---

* The SWP working group has enlisted a number of voices and comments, mainly from practitioners of diplomacy, which are highly pertinent to the issue of how diplomacy evolves in the 21st century. The following is a contribution by Karsten D. Voigt, a former member of the German Bundestag, a member of the NATO Parliamentary Assembly, and a German-American Coordinator in the Federal Foreign Office.

the solution of the problem. In Europe, Berlin will very often be one of the involved capitals.

Due to Germany's weight, Berlin will in the future communicate even more with other capitals as well as with EU institutions. However, simply because of time constraints, it will not always be possible to equally inform all member states of the EU. German diplomacy is aware of this problem and therefore endeavours to include particularly the smaller EU member states during the process, or at least afterwards. This inclusive effort mitigates the problem of asymmetrical influence between larger and smaller states, but is not enough to solve it.

New forms of communication such as email, video calls, and direct messaging, the overall reinforced intensity of communication, as well as time constraints all lead to an increase in verbal exchange outside of formal reporting channels, especially in times of crisis. The availability of new communication pathways changes the mode of operation within foreign ministries and with the chancellery as well as among other ministries. Within the EU it changes in particular the role of embassies. During immediate and time-sensitive cases, communication increasingly takes place directly between capitals. Consequently, bilateral embassies in EU member states have become ever more marginalised participants in these processes, or are not involved at all. This leads to a change in the functioning of embassies within the EU: on the one hand, they increasingly accompany direct negotiations between governments, on the other hand, they partially undertake what traditionally has been staff work. In this way, they prepare the talks contentwise, as was previously done by the ministries' bureaus.

2. *New Competencies at the Top Operational Level*

Within the EU, heads of government, foreign ministers, and specialized ministers meet frequently. Not merely the formal meetings of heads of government or specialized ministers, but also the numerous other formal and informal bi- and multilateral meetings. At these meetings opinions are expressed and agreements are reached that relativize the coordinating function of the foreign ministries in European affairs. Whether a transfer of the coordinating role of the foreign ministry to the chancellery would solve the problem or only relocate it needs to be determined in the future. It is conceivable that as a result, work on substance – particularly in the most politically important areas – will also be drawn into the realm of the chancellery.

3. *Interministerial Exchange in the European Union*

In addition, all relevant federal ministries in Germany have established task forces concerning international and European policy aspects of their ministries. Staff members in these task forces are often 'borrowed' from the foreign ministry. However, the fact of having personnel from the foreign ministry does not prevent individual ministries from developing direct working relations with their partners in other European capitals and at the EU level. This influences the substantive work as well and complicates the effectiveness of national coordination of the European policy by the foreign ministry. Official representation of federal states at the EU is functioning similarly.

4. *The Impact of European 'Party Families'*

All parties represented in the German Bundestag belong to European associations of similar and/or like-minded parties. In the case of the newly created *Alternative for Germany* (AfD) Europe-wide coordination of anti-European parties has only just begun. Many of these parties belong to parliaments or governments on national levels. Often, members of the European Commission proclaim their affiliation to one of these 'party families.' Most parties in the European Parliament regard themselves as a parliamentary arm of such a 'party family.'

The role of party associations on the European level is significantly weaker than the role of national parties. However, party associations are effective as transnational networks and as instruments giving still predominantly national politics a transnational frame. They particularly influence personnel decisions at the European Commission and other European institutions. In that respect, national and European politicians can exert influence in this area.

Thanks to their functions in their parties, heads of government, foreign ministries, and leading opposition politicians are frequently involved in these European networks. Diplomats are often affected by the agreements thus made, but are seldom involved and sometimes insufficiently informed. Although the politicization of civil service can thereby (rightly) be avoided, it may happen that diplomats learn too late about such agreements, and so miss out on knowledge essential for their analyses, reports, and recommendations. Due to the informal nature of these kinds of meetings and agreements, so far very few studies have examined their role.

5. The 'Nebenaußenpolitik' (Parallel Foreign Policy) of Parties

In Germany, in the context of the conflict concerning the NATO Double-Track Decision in the decade before the fall of the Berlin Wall, there was a public dispute regarding what was then called 'Nebenaußenpolitik' (parallel foreign policy) by the Social Democratic Party. This referred to the co-operation between Social Democratic Parties in Scandinavia, the Benelux countries, and Germany (so-called Euro-Lux or Scandia-Lux), among other things. It served as a coordinating platform for the parties' position regarding the NATO Double-Track Decision, and subsequent negotiations between the United States and the Soviet Union. Transnational coordination of foreign and security policy through parties is often at odds with the political intentions of respective national governments. However, such transnational processes may be considered part of the logic of an increasing and a legitimate convergence between member states of the EU. With the decreasing role of large political parties and the dissolution of party affiliation amongst the electorate in general, the 'Nebenaußenpolitik' by parties seems to be replaced more and more by a similar process with other actors such as NGOs (for example, their role concerning the U.N. 2030 Agenda for Sustainable Development). Therefore, 'Nebenaußenpolitik' in a much wider sense might well be a future-orientated element of German and European foreign policy, which corresponds with the multiplication of actors, who all exert their influence on foreign policy.

6. The Influence of National Parliaments

Finally: Foreign policy is traditionally seen as the prerogative of the executive branch. Academically, the influence of parliaments is often assessed with reference to the division between executive and legislative branches along the lines prescribed by state constitutions. The prerogatives of parliaments constitute their 'hard power.'

However, beyond that they also possess 'soft power': their influence on political opinion-building. This is true of the German Bundestag and also applies to the still undervalued European Parliament. It even extends to the Parliamentary Assembly of the Council of Europe, although that still has limited competences.

There is only one institution in the transatlantic relationship whereby members of parliament on both sides of the Atlantic can regularly meet for an intense dialogue regarding foreign and security policy issues: the Parliamentary Assembly of NATO. It has no competences, but might be used in the future for influencing political opinion-building in the parliaments of the member states of NATO – a role it has occasionally assumed in the past.

One outstanding concrete example demonstrates how the Parliamentary Assembly can exert influence. Several years before the German Federal Government and the U.S. Administration agreed upon the enlargement of NATO to the East, and long before a majority for it emerged in the U.S. Congress and the German Bundestag, Volker Rühe and others endorsed the NATO enlargement to the East. All of them campaigned for it in Europe and in the United States, creating a task force focusing on the substance of a concept for NATO enlargement, and drafting different models of NATO, including the question of the deployment of troops and nuclear weapons. It was sent to all relevant parliaments in Eastern Europe, including Russia, which surprisingly responded. A discussion continued in this way for several years, pre-empting later decisions by the concerned governments, and impacting on much later decisions by governments, parliaments, and even parties, in relevant if not measurable ways. The strengthening role of national parliaments in the diplomacy of their countries is thus something new, and governments benefit from contributions coming from different perspectives.

*

Diplomacy needs to recognize problems and courses of action early on while also seeking creative and target-oriented ways to develop tools for shaping foreign policy. Today, this can be achieved by actors, at least within the scope of the EU, who previously hardly touched foreign policy: national parliaments, parties, new European 'party families,' other ministries beside the foreign ministry, heads of state and governments (who take responsibilities from the ministries of foreign affairs) – and, although less and less, the embassies within the European states.

The parties involved in this process of shaping foreign policy – predominantly bureaucrats and politicians – are not yet completely aware of this development. It is possible that diplomats are thus not yet adequately prepared for these changes. But one thing is certain: the foreign ministries must prepare for the consequences of an emerging need to deal with new, increasingly influential actors when they revise their structures and procedures.

The Domestic Challenges of European Geoeconomic Diplomacy

Kim B. Olsen

The strategic utilisation of economic, monetary or financial capabilities to advance their own geopolitical objectives has, in historic terms, been a defining aspect of almost every geographical entity's foreign policy behaviour.[1] For diplomatic practitioners, the interplay between governments and markets, and its impact on the former's room for manoeuvre on the international stage, remains a fundamental tenet that is of analytical importance. For scholars of international political economy, economic statecraft, economic foreign policy and the like, the relationship between wealth and power is a core driver of theoretical debate and innovation. In light of the remarkable structural fluidity that defines the 21st century's 'multipolarised' global economy[2] – where unprecedented levels of interconnectedness and rapid redistributions of wealth from traditionally prosperous Western states to the Global South has resulted in the economic empowerment of an increasing number of major global powers – even broader foreign affairs audiences have recently developed interest in how the sphere of macroeconomics directly affects conditions of modern foreign policy making. Particular interest lies with how economically powerful states instrumentalise sources of economic power as incentivising or coercing measures to foster their foreign policy interests. Such targeted use of economic capabilities, or geoeconomic instruments, range from economic sanction regimes, to trade and investment policies over financial and monetary policies, to politically driven economic assistance, to policies governing energy and commodities, as well as some forms of cyber instruments.[3] Diplomats, both in Europe and beyond, thus find themselves increasingly exposed to a diplomatic field that can be described as *geoeconomic diploma-*

1 David A. Baldwin, *Economic Statecraft* (Princeton, NJ: Princeton University Press, 1985).

2 Oliver Stuenkel, *Post-Western World: How Emerging Powers Are Remaking Global Order* (Malden, MA: Polity Press, 2016).

3 Robert D. Blackwill and Jennifer M. Harris, *War by Other Means: Geoeconomics and Statecraft* (Cambridge, MA: The Belknap Press of Harvard University Press, 2016).

cy, which is understood as the realm where a government is willing and able to employ national economic capabilities to preserve and realise its national interests when conducting relationships with other international actors.[4]

If modern foreign policy making is shaped by states' abilities to mobilise economic resources as a pertinent source of power, one could be tempted to argue that Europe's position as a 'military dwarf but an economic giant' per se should give it a competitive advantage in the geoeconomic playing field. This chapter warns against such premature conclusions, and suggests that the existence of material wealth does not in itself suffice for a government's ability to translate its economic capabilities into tangible foreign policy and diplomatic tools. In short, in the field of geoeconomic diplomacy money alone cannot secure influence.

In this chapter, I therefore argue that any government's ability to employ geoeconomic instruments is not merely a function of means (a state's economic resources) and ends (the advancement of its national interests), but heavily depends on its diplomats' ability to work in concert with various influential domestic governmental and non-governmental actors. This is particularly important in liberal market economies, where a plethora of mostly non-governmental actors often hold or influence substantial parts of those national economic resources that governmental foreign policy makers might want to instrumentalise for foreign policy purposes. At the same time, these actors operate largely independently from direct governmental control. In the context of EU foreign policy making, this perspective shows us how Europe's geoeconomic impact is not only limited by the daunting task of finding alignment between the national interests of 28 member state governments, but also the challenges governments face to continuously operate and collaborate with non-governmental actors at the domestic level.

A nuanced understanding of such structural conditions becomes even more important when considering that recent global redistributions of material wealth has in the meantime exposed and emphasised certain ideational variations among powerful states – i.e. the 'multiple poles.' Chi-

4 The notion of geoeconomics presented here is inspired by the one presented by Blackwill and Harris, *War by Other Means* (see note 3), and thus sides with the first of two 'traditions' in the geoeconomics literature: i) the effects of economic policies on national power and geopolitics ('the flag follows trade') or ii) the economic consequences of the projection of national power ('trade follows the flag') (Sanjaya Baru, "Geo-economics and Strategy", *Survival* 54, no. 3 [June 2012]: 47–58).

na, India and (to a lesser extent) Russia have been among the last decades' most successful competitors in the global race to align economic wealth with geopolitical objectives. These rising powers also represent governance models where governments have significant influence over national economic assets or hold substantial ownership stakes in major domestic companies – leverage that in turn can be utilised for strategic foreign policy purposes, e.g. by directly interfering in strategically vital economic sectors of rivalling major economies.[5] This global return of 'state capitalism'[6] thus highlights another pivotal challenge for European diplomats engaged in quests of transposing the interplay between governments and markets to the arena of geopolitics.

These substantial points have so far been largely neglected by the geoeconomic literature, since it has failed to acknowledge that the mere existence of a country's economic power does not automatically translate into the applicability of specific geoeconomic instruments in a state's diplomatic practice. As suggested by Sascha Lohmann in this volume, the role of diplomats in applying geoeconomic instruments, such as sanctions, remains significantly understudied. In addressing these theoretical fallacies, this chapter argues that a network-based analytical approach can help to obtain more nuanced understandings of the domestic relationships and challenges European diplomats and ministries of foreign affairs (MFAs) face in the geoeconomic sphere. Such a refined perspective could help to better assess – and ultimately improve – European governments' engagements in one of the early 21st century's most critical diplomatic playing fields.

---

5 Joshua Kurlantzick, *State Capitalism: How the Return of Statism Is Transforming the World* (New York: Oxford University Press, 2016), 9; Maaike Okano-Heijmans, "Conceptualizing Economic Diplomacy: The Crossroads of International Relations, Economics, IPE and Diplomatic Studies", *The Hague Journal of Diplomacy* 6, no. 1 (January 2011): 7–36.

6 The somewhat bold contrast between 'state capitalism' and 'liberal market economies' depicts ideal types of varying modes of economic governance rather than nuanced empirical descriptions of state-market relations. Though most powerful economies will find elements of both models in their everyday governance structures (depending on the economic sector in question), governments' general understanding of proper levels of state-market independence does vary substantially enough to utilise this juxtaposition for analytical purposes.

From Sanctions to Free Trade Agreements: Geoeconomics on the Rise in EU Foreign Policy Making

A strengthened debate about the conditions for European geoeconomic diplomacy is paramount in the current context, where central aspects underpinning the EU's Common Foreign and Security Policy (CFSP) are driven by the utilisation of economic capabilities. Prominent examples include the strategic use of economic integration agreements (EIAs)[7] and economic sanction regimes – both of which in recent years have been among the most popular instruments in the EU's foreign policy toolbox – to foster wider geopolitical interests.

Firstly, the extensive and growing list of European EIAs with third countries does not only reflect the EU's economic ambitions in the realm of international trade, but also, as various recent cases illustrate, how negotiations on free trade and customs unions often hold broader strategic, geopolitical dimensions. The rapid deterioration of trade negotiations between the EU and the United States moving from near finalisation of the Transatlantic Trade and Investment Partnership (TTIP) in 2016 – envisaged by some policy makers as an 'economic NATO'[8] – to recent announcements by President Trump in spring 2018 of imposing tariffs on imports of steel and aluminium, has led to widespread concerns over a looming 'trade warfare' on both sides of the Atlantic.

A similar link between trade and geopolitical antagonisms was pivotal in the EU's negotiations about Association Agreements and Deep and Comprehensive Free Trade Areas (AA/DCFTA) with the Eastern Partnership (EP) countries. Even as EU officials persistently downplayed geopolitical objectives as a driver for bringing EP countries closer to the EU's internal market, the Russian government's overtly sceptical and aggressive reactions to the final negotiation stages between the EU and, particularly, Ukraine in late 2013 – and the events that led to the 'Ukrainian crisis' – suggest that this benign view of Brussels was not shared in Moscow.

Secondly, the EU-Russian spat over Ukraine likewise constitutes an arena for the EU's use of economic sanctions, another 'popular' geoeconomic instrument. European preference for utilising this geoeconomic instrument has been on the rise since the so-called 'sanctions decade' of the

7 Defined as a common term for partial or full free trade agreements (FTAs), preferential trade agreements (PTAs), or customs unions.

8 Jennifer M. Harris, "America, Europe and the Necessary Geopolitics of Trade", *Survival* 58, no. 6 (December 2016): 63–92.

1990's, resulting in a situation where the EU currently upholds around 35 sanctions regimes ranging from asset freezes and travel bans against listed individuals to trade embargos and financial restrictions against targeted countries.[9] Following the Russian annexation of Crimea in spring 2014 and the downing of flight MH17 over Ukraine (allegedly by Russian-backed rebels) in summer 2014, EU member states responded with a comprehensive listing of individuals and commercial entities with links to the government in Moscow. Russia was thereby added to the list of countries targeted by European sanctions for geopolitical purposes; a list that already features the nuclear programmes of Iran and North Korea as other prominent examples in this category.

Interestingly, more conceptually driven discussions about the intersection of economic power and foreign policy goals, and how to cope with them in organisational terms, have reached Brussels where the notion of a European 'economic diplomacy' has lately been making its rounds.[10] Though such discussions mostly aim at the use of political power to foster European economic interests than vice-versa, it is encouraging that the strategic focus on the state-market nexus is gaining attention. In institutional terms, such discussions could – and should – also translate into more strategic debates and coordination between various EU council formats relating to international affairs. It is for instance telling that coordination between the Foreign Affairs Council (FAC) and its economic 'sister councils', FAC Trade and FAC Development, still remains rather rudimentary according to practitioners in the field.

---

9 Manuel Lafont Rapnouil, "Signal, Constrain, and Coerce: A More Strategic Use of Sanctions", in *The New European Security Initiative*, ed. Ulrike Esther Franke, Manuel Lafont Rapnouil and Susi Dennison (London: European Council on Foreign Relations, December 2017), 28–30.

10 Brian Hocking, Jan Melissen, Shaun Riordan and Paul Sharp, *Whither Foreign Ministries in a Post-Western World?*, Clingendael Policy Brief, no. 20 (The Hague: Netherlands Institute of International Relations 'Clingendael', April 2013); Maaike Okano-Heijmans and Francesco Saverio Montesano, *Who Is Afraid of European Economic Diplomacy?*, Clingendael Policy Brief (The Hague: Netherlands Institute of International Relations 'Clingendael', April 2016).

The Neglected Foreign Policy Role of Non-Governmental Agency in Europe's Liberal Market Economies

Scrutinising the role of domestic structures in shaping governments' room for manoeuvre in the geoeconomic diplomatic realm seems particularly important in the European context. Here Blackwill and Harris have interestingly noted that indeed "today's form of geoeconomics comes with not only new options but also new diplomatic tools."[11] However, the real significance of this observation lies in their subsequent caveat stating that "some of these [geoeconomic] instruments are […] largely unavailable to U.S. and Western leaders."[12] Though the authors do not substantiate their claim further, this unavailability relates to the relative independence of market actors from direct governmental interference in liberal market economies, where economic power is largely in the hands of private actors. The use of geoeconomic instruments thereby differs greatly from that of military instruments, which are under the control of civilian governmental and military actors alone. These specificities of the geoeconomic playing fields potentially offer far reaching consequences for European diplomacy, particularly because similar structural limitations do not seem as pertinent for governments in countries with stronger state capitalist structures.

In sum, European leaders and diplomats' limited access to the economic capabilities that could be instrumentalised for geopolitical purposes therefore arises either because diplomats do not themselves possess the economic lever needed to set the given geoeconomic instrument in play, or that they are dependent on non-governmental or international organisations to implement it. The former situation, for example, arises when governments seek to impose instruments by adopting legal frameworks that impact trade relations through EIAs or sanctions. Such legal frameworks will only be efficient if they are loyally implemented by businesses actors and other government representatives. The latter situation, for example, relates to states' instrumental use of economic assistance – ranging from short-term stabilisation funds to long-term development assistance – where implementation often can only be properly executed with significant assistance from implementing partners on the ground (United Nations, NGOs, companies etc.). What adds to the complexity is that many of such non-governmental actors often have their own capacities to perform independently at the international level; such agency potentially acts in a manner that un-

11 Blackwill and Harris, *War by Other Means* (see note 3), 9–10.

12 Ibid.

dermines a government's foreign policy agenda. Particularly in the European context such non-state actors therefore play pivotal roles in determining the foreign policy options that diplomats enjoy at the international level. Academic and policy-oriented discussions about the future of diplomacy will have to take this dynamic into account in a systemised and serious manner.

The Fallacies of Structuralism for Understanding Geoeconomic Diplomacy

Looking at the recent scholarly debate about geoeconomics, however, it is striking that such actor- and organisational-level perspectives are rarely taken properly into account in a literature that is overtly dominated by structuralist approaches which largely neglect the relationalism inherent in everyday diplomacy, and thereby prevents in-depth thinking about the *diplomatic* aspects of geoeconomics.[13] Much of this literature is centred around system-level assumptions – with an intellectual legacy from both neorealism and neomercantilism – that seeks to remind us that states' increased use of economic means in an inherently unstable multipolar international system more often leads to inter-state antagonism and conflict. Therefore, current scholarly debate about geoeconomics remains limited in its scope, since it often rests on the un-nuanced assumption that governments are able to translate economic wealth into international power through rational interest maximisation.[14]

This analytical insensibility towards the nuts and bolts of the geoeconomic field also bears normative consequences. Structuralist accounts over-emphasise how governments' sheer use of geoeconomic instruments leads to the 'weaponisation of economies' or even 'wars by other means'.[15] The gloomiest of such accounts was expressed by Luttwak in his (in)fa-

13 Rebecca Adler-Nissen, "Conclusion: Relationalism or Why Diplomats find International Relations Theory Strange", in *Diplomacy and the Making of World Politics*, ed. Ole Jacob Sending, Vincent Pouliot and Iver B. Neumann (Cambridge: Cambridge University Press, 2015), 284–308.

14 Blackwill and Harris, *War by Other Means* (see note 3); Mikael Wigell, "Conceptualizing Regional Powers' Geoeconomic Strategies: Neo-Imperialism, Neo-Mercantilism, and Liberal Institutionalism", *Asia Europe Journal* 14, no. 2 (June 2016): 135–51.

15 Blackwill and Harris, *War by Other Means* (see note 3); Mark Leonard, "Introduction: Connectivity Wars", in *Connectivity Wars: Why Migration, Finance and Trade are the Geo-Economic Battlegrounds of the Future*, ed. Mark Leonard (London: European Council on Foreign Relations, January 2016), 13–27.

mous dictum describing geoeconomics as "the logic of conflict with the grammar of commerce."[16] While such theoretical warnings are not necessarily futile, this chapter questions the determinism embedded in these structural approaches and calls for more nuanced reflections on how diplomats' relationships with various domestic actors can affect a government's ability to utilise the geoeconomic instrument it might seek to.

In solely analysing the geoeconomic playing field at the structural level, current debates fall short of understanding the politico-economic conditions and limitations that European policy makers face, and hence tend to underestimate the impact of actor-specific relationships on governments' interests, negotiating positions and outcomes. If these conditions are not carefully analysed in relationship to the specific state-market context, as well as the particular geoeconomic instrument in question (sanctions, EIAs, economic assistance etc.), scholarly debates about European geoeconomics will remain detached from a realistic understanding of the conditions diplomats face in the geoeconomic field.

Shifting Perspective: From 'Diplomatic Systems' to 'Diplomatic Networks'

Considering in a systemised way the role of domestic actors in foreign policy making, such as is prevalent in a great deal of literature on Foreign Policy Analysis and diplomacy studies, is in itself obviously far from being a novel approach. Works on 'multi-stakeholder diplomacy',[17] 'national diplomatic systems',[18] and 'network diplomacy'[19] have been particularly helpful in highlighting the importance of treating the behaviour and interests of

---

16 Edward N. Luttwak, "From Geopolitics to Geo-Economics: Logic of Conflict, Grammar of Commerce", *The National Interest* 20 (Summer 1990): 17–23; David Criekemans, "Where Geoeconomics and Geostrategy Meet: The Troubled Relations between the European Union and the Russian Federation", in *Advances in Geoeconomics*, ed. J. Mark Munoz (London and New York: Routledge, 2017), 113–20.

17 Brian Hocking, "Multistakeholder Diplomacy: Forms, Functions, and Frustrations", in *Multistakeholder Diplomacy – Challenges and Opportunities*, ed. Jovan Kurbalija and Valentin Katrandjiev (Geneva: DiploFoundation, 2006), 13–29.

18 Brian Hocking, "The Ministry of Foreign Affairs and the National Diplomatic System", in *Diplomacy in a Globalizing World: Theories and Practices*, ed. Pauline Kerr and Geoffrey Wiseman (New York: Oxford University Press, 2013), 123–40.

19 Jorge Heine, "From Club to Network Diplomacy", in *The Oxford Handbook of Modern Diplomacy*, ed. Andrew F. Cooper, Jorge Heine and Ramesh Thakur (Oxford: Oxford University Press, 2013), 54–69.

domestic actors as vital aspects of modern diplomacy. Some of these contributions furthermore echo the 'second image' IR debates from the 1970–90s where scholars such as Katzenstein, Putnam and Moravcsik proposed various rationalistic explanations for the importance of domestic actors and structures in forming a state's foreign policy interests and negotiation behaviour at the European or international level.[20] Yet neither these classic studies, nor more recent 'updates' of their analytical frameworks, present coherent tools for the careful scrutiny of relationships between 'traditional' MFA diplomats with other governmental and, particularly, non-governmental actors in the geoeconomic field. As such, they do not provide insights into how the everyday practices that form relationships with these domestic actors influence a state's diplomatic behaviour at the international level.

Instead of understanding the relationship between the government and domestic actors as a rational bargaining game[21] at the domestic level, which then determines a government's position at the international level (and vice versa), I propose thinking about these relationships as a plethora of social ties linked via networks that in various degrees influences a government's diplomatic behaviour. Hocking has pointed in this direction by introducing the notion of a 'National Diplomatic System' (NDS) that emphasises how the internationalisation of national ministries and governmental agencies has for some time challenged the roles of MFAs as their government's diplomatic face.[22] While there is certainly plenty of empiri-

---

20 Peter J. Katzenstein, "International Relations and Domestic Structures: Foreign Economic Policies of Advanced Industrial States", *International Organization* 30, no. 1 (Winter 1976): 1–45; Robert D. Putnam, "Diplomacy and Domestic Politics: The Logic of Two-Level Games", *International Organization* 42, no. 3 (Summer 1988): 427–60; Andrew Moravcsik, "Liberal Intergovernmentalism and Integration: A Rejoinder", *Journal of Common Market Studies* 33, no. 4 (December 1995): 611–28.

21 The idea of bargaining games (a central tenet of e.g. Putnam and Moravcsik's theorising) implies that negotiators are a priori aware of their priorities and win-sets, even though these can be said to develop in the process of domestic consultation and international negotiation – a process that furthermore may not be sequential. With reference to the notion of "circum-negotiation" (Harold Saunders, "Prenegotiation and Circum-negotiation: Arenas of the Peace Process", in *Managing Global Chaos*, ed. Chester A. Crocker, Fen Osler Hampson and Pamela Aall [Washington, D.C.: United States Institute of Peace Press, 1996], 419–32), one should be aware that diplomats and other actors may change their interests in the context of unfolding domestic and international relationships and, critically, in the course of negotiations.

22 Hocking, "The Ministry of Foreign Affairs" (see note 18).

cal evidence supporting this development, I argue that the specific nature of geoeconomic diplomacy necessitates analytical frameworks that (1) also encompass the substantial roles played by domestic non-governmental actors and (2) allows for greater sensibility towards how the involvement of such actors changes from case to case and thus for a less static understanding of unfolding relationships and cooperation than Hocking's notion of 'systems' calls for.

I argue that insights from the rapidly growing literature on network theory in IR could serve as a viable bridge in building such analytical frameworks. While space does not permit elaborating extensively on these ideas here, a first analytical move could be to place the MFA as a central node in networks constituted through its multiple relationships with governmental and non-governmental actors. Analysing the practices within such networks could help to identify domestic actors that either strengthen or weaken the MFA's ability to utilise a given geoeconomic instrument.[23] Even if the placement of the MFA as the central network actor is not necessarily an accurate empirical reflection of an MFA's centrality in all aspects of a state's foreign relations, this *analytical* move would help to better determine how 'traditional' MFA diplomats relate to relevant governmental and non-governmental actors – and how these relations impact a country's abilities to operate in the geoeconomic diplomatic field.[24]

---

23 Following the seminal definition of Hafner-Burton et al., I understand networks as any set or sets of ties between any set or sets of nodes. Network analysis, then, "concerns relationships defined by links among nodes (or agents) [and] addresses the associations among nodes rather than the attributes of particular nodes" (Emilie M. Hafner-Burton, Miles Kahler and Alexander H. Montgomery, "Network Analysis for International Relations", *International Organization* 63, no. 3 [July 2009]: 559–92 [562]).

24 By granting the state a central role in my analytical framework, my approach differs from that of the emerging research agenda on transnational, cross-border networks and new forms of global governance in networks beyond the national state (Miles Kahler, ed., *Networked Politics: Agency, Power, and Governance* [Ithaca: Cornell University Press, 2009]; Anne-Marie Slaughter, *The Chessboard and the Web – Strategies of Connection in a Networked World* [New Haven, CT, and London: Yale University Press, 2017]).

Making European Sanctions Work? The Role of German Domestic Networks in the EU's Sanction Regime against Russia

The aforementioned European economic sanctions against Russia serve as an illustrative case for the practical implications that such a network-based approach could have for unpacking the domestic challenges European diplomats face in the geoeconomic playing field. In spring and summer 2014, the EU adopted substantial sanction regimes in response to Russia's illegal annexation of the Crimean Peninsula and the downing of flight MH17 over Ukraine. While the former Russian move led to asset freezes and visa bans for individuals, the latter incident resulted in general economic sanctions adopted by the EU Council in July 2014, essentially banning much economic activity with the Russian banking, energy and military sectors.

Analysts have described how the potentially divisive question of imposing significant, strong economic sanctions against Russia has yet not torpedoed EU consensus on the matter. At the same time, pro-sanction advocates, such as Germany and France, were yet again faced with significant opposition by member states less inclined to follow the hardnosed approach against Moscow.[25]

This intergovernmental bargaining dynamic is a well-known characteristic of EU foreign policy making. The importance of these state-to-state negotiations notwithstanding, the realm of geoeconomics invites for an expanded and nuanced understanding of the dynamics diplomats need to take into consideration. Using a network-based approach can help to shed light on how the European use of economic sanctions against Russia has been challenged and influenced by various domestic actors – among them some that would normally not show overt interest in EU foreign policy decisions, as well as those who came to see themselves as most negatively affected by the sanction-related trade and financial restrictions. While space does not permit a thorough analysis of the circumstances leading to the formulation, adoption and implementation of the sanctions regime, some brief reflections on the domestic challenges faced by the German MFA, a

25 For a good overview see Mitchell A. Orenstein and R. Daniel Kelemen, "Trojan Horses in EU Foreign Policy", *Journal of Common Market Studies* 55, no. 1 (January 2017): 87–102.

leading actor in this process,[26] will highlight the structural conditions for viewing sanctions instruments through a network-oriented lens.

From the outset, the Ukraine crisis hit a political nerve among Berlin's policy makers, who were already troubled by questions over whether the guiding principles behind the German Russia policy were still adequate.[27] Perceiving the German MFA as the network centre helps to identify a wide range of involved domestic actors, from other ministries and members of both the federal and regional parliaments, to business organisations and major companies, to former statesmen, who each put pressure on the German MFA and influenced its room for manoeuvre when negotiating and implementing the sanctions regime in the years 2014 to 2016. Here are some primary examples:

a) Government agencies: The German MFA was subject to dual pressure from other leading governmental agencies. On the one hand, Chancellor Merkel and her Chancellery were actively engaged in the sanction negotiations from a very early stage of the conflict, while promoting a sturdier and more confrontational line towards Moscow than that preferred by the SPD-led MFA. Although the Chancellery is regularly involved in major foreign policy decisions, the potential losses for major German business interests as well as the geopolitical dimensions at play here raised the political stakes significantly. At times the lack of policy coherence between the Chancellery and the MFA – particularly in the early formulation phase of the EU sanction regime – led diplomats from other European member states to question whose policy line represented the 'real' German position. On the other hand, the Ministry of Economics, both in internal discussions and public statements, repeatedly spoke in favour of a progressive dismantlement of sanctions at a faster pace than that envisioned by the MFA, thereby reflecting demands both from parts of the SPD party base and the mood in the German business community. This duality continually challenged the MFA's role as the unified voice of the German government in negotiations with other European partners and the Russian government.

---

26 Though the EU sanctions regime was unanimously adopted by all EU member states, Germany – together with France – came to play a pivotal role in the EU's negotiations with Russia and Ukraine in the so-called Normandy Format.

27 Tuoamas Forsberg, "From Ostpolitik to 'Frostpolitik'? Merkel, Putin and German Foreign Policy towards Russia", *International Affairs* 92, no. 1 (January 2016): 21–42; Marco Siddi, "German Foreign Policy towards Russia in the Aftermath of the Ukraine Crisis: A New *Ostpolitik?*", *Europe-Asia Studies* 68, no. 4 (June 2016): 665–77.

b) Business community: As a major representative of the German business community, the Federation of German Industries (BDI) publicly spoke out in favour of the sanctions at an early stage, which was helpful for Germany's diplomatic endeavour. Although the BDI's positive stance was challenged internally by its sub-federation for large German businesses with interest in the Russian and east European markets – the German Committee on Eastern European Economic Relations (OA) – the BDI's backing helped the MFA to strengthen its network position towards a somewhat sceptical German business community who feared substantial losses in their trade relations with Russia. Although there is little evidence that German businesses acted as overt 'sanction spoilers', cases such as the deliverance of gas turbines from the German company Siemens to sanctioned Crimea (arguably against Siemens' knowledge) demonstrate how governments' implementation of sanctions can be hampered by legal loopholes and complex production and delivery chains.

c) Regional government level: Another domestic pressure was apparent from the regional government level when Bavaria's Prime Minister Seehofer visited Russian President Putin in February 2016. Without the direct consent of the German government, Seehofer promoted a more benign stance on the sanction question than the federal government's official line. Seehofer's visit was most likely a signal to Bavarian small- and medium-sized enterprises, who had vocally expressed their discomfort at negative exposure to the effects of both EU sanctions and Russian counter-sanctions. The German business community's impact was thus tangible on multiple governmental levels.

In sum, while German diplomats found themselves placed at the forefront of the EU's negotiations with, and targeting of economic sanctions against, Russia, the network perspective helps to highlight how the German MFA had to allocate substantial resources to navigate a network of domestic actors in order to secure coherent access to the economic-based leverage so deeply needed in the geoeconomic confrontation with Russia. Such continuous and greatly varying domestic challenges are tangible examples of the complexities facing diplomats that seek to mobilise economic instruments which ultimately are not exclusively under their control.

Concluding remarks

The competencies that diplomats need to operate at the interface between foreign policy, economics and business were at the heart of a significant speech by U.S. Secretary of State Hillary Clinton in 2011, when she declared that the future would bring great demand for diplomats that can "read both Foreign Affairs and a Bloomberg Terminal."[28] Clinton's essential message was clear: understanding and handling the geoeconomic sphere is not only key for diplomats dealing with trade negotiations (trade diplomacy) or helping domestic businesses to succeed in foreign markets (commercial diplomacy), but also for those handling 'classic' security-related and geopolitical issues.

Such reflections on the special nature of geoeconomic diplomacy obviously relate to more general discussions about the agency of non-governmental actors in modern diplomacy. As the field of geoeconomics becomes ever more important for foreign policy makers across the globe, demands for European diplomacy and diplomats are changing rapidly. The traditional state-to-state understanding of diplomacy is deteriorating, and new analytical frameworks that encompass the 'networked' relationship between MFAs with other governmental and non-governmental actors still need to be developed and discussed.

As shown in the illustrative case of German MFA's domestic challenges when aiming for a common EU sanction regime against Russia, economic sanctions – unlike other foreign policy tools – can have direct economic impacts on domestic business communities, which not only leads to potential inter-agency turf battles, but also gives domestic actors incentives for trying to circumvent their own government's policies. This requires diplomats to navigate in highly volatile domestic environments – and analysts that work in the field of geoeconomics to be sensitive towards the unpredictability and complexity of such domestic networks.

Bagger and von Heynitz advanced a similar view when elaborating on the idea of 'the networked diplomat' who should be able to integrate external ideas as well as interests from a wide range of government and non-government actors.[29] Fletcher's ideas about the necessity for the modern 'naked diplomat' to operate in rapidly changing and unforeseeable circumstances among a plethora of actors in the 'real' and digital realm moves in a similar direction.[30] While these observations help to sharpen our sensitivity

---

28 Hillary R. Clinton, "Economic Statecraft", Speech at the Economic Club of New York, New York City, 14 October 2011, https://2009-2017.state.gov/secretary/20092013clinton/rm/2011/10/175552.htm (accessed 24 July 2018).

29 Thomas Bagger and Wolfram von Heynitz, "Der vernetzte Diplomat: Von vernetzter Sicherheit zu einer „netzwerkorientierten Außenpolitik", *Zeitschrift für Außen- und Sicherheitspolitik* 5, no. 1 (October 2012): 49–61.

30 Tom Fletcher, *The Naked Diplomat: Power and Statecraft in the Digital Century* (London: William Collins, 2016).

to dynamics on the changing playing field of modern diplomacy, they do not suffice as coherent answers to key questions in the field of geoeconomics. Some of the most relevant issues for further research concern under *which* circumstances domestic actors influence a government's access to various geoeconomic instruments, *how* these domestic actors enact this influence and *what* this 'networked reality' means for the leeway that European foreign policy making can have on the international stage. In addition, while this paper has shed light on the domestic dynamics that diplomats face in the geoeconomic realm, the often complex relationships with international (non-government) actors should likewise receive careful attention when searching for answers to these and similar questions – and which will remain paramount for diplomats and diplomacy scholars in the early 21st century.

Autism in Foreign Policy

Hanns W. Maull

In this volume the definition of 'diplomacy' has at its core the pursuit of the enlightened self-interests of politically organized collectives[1] in and through their interaction with others, as well as with other international actors, such as non-governmental organizations or transnational corporations. Diplomacy, as the conduct of foreign policy, will therefore be a key resource for making world politics – and the world itself – sustainably peaceful. Diplomats thus represent *polities*; diplomacy concerns *politics*, in other words, the way the international realm is governed; and diplomacy must find and implement *policies* that are able to realize specific collective aims and, beyond that, the productive co-habitation of all states and peoples.

What Diplomacy Needs to Deliver: Changing Demands on Governance beyond the State

Both the conduct of national politics and the capacity of states to develop and implement policies within an overall framework of orientation (a national 'grand strategy' or 'role concept'), appear worldwide to be undergoing profound transformations as a result of two major forces: the trajectory of technological change and the revolution of rising expectations among peoples. *Technological change*, driven by the advances of scientific knowledge and their application for the practical purposes of problem-solving and the gratification of human desires, has produced exponential growth in all kinds of social interactions within and across borders. We call this 'globalization'. Globalization has deepened the interdependence between individuals and societies, and will continue to do so in the future, quite possibly at an even more accelerated pace.

Globalization has also transformed the state and will continue to do so: the requirements that an effective functioning state has to meet are a mov-

1 Usually, this would be states or state-like entities, or international organizations that represent states.

ing target which more and more states (having often been 'quasi-states' to begin with)[2] now find it difficult to meet. As a result, they may become 'failing' or even 'failed' states.

That same logic also operates beyond the nation state. Enhanced interdependence has transformed the requirements for governance beyond the state and will continue thus in the future. In fact, the logic of technological change seems to demand governance, and therefore international politics, of a density and quality that so far has been largely confined to politics *within* a state.

At the same time, domestic politics itself is changing under the transformative impact of globalization. In practice, challenges usually take the form of political demands addressed by citizens or groups to their political leaders. These demands merge into the second secular trend affecting diplomacy in the 21st century: the *revolution of rising expectations*. Expectations concern material benefits as well as normative or ideological aspirations. The dominant forces driving collective expectations today are the promise of material growth and the ideology of what Yuval Harari calls "humanism": the centrality of the individual in our conceptions of society.[3] Both forces are expansive. Additionally, there are the growing number of people cramming into the world and the rising levels of individual empowerment through education and knowledge. Consequently, expectations are rising rapidly, and quite possibly exponentially. Again, this puts pressure on politics, within and between states.

What Diplomacy Can Deliver: The Constraints of Sovereignty

The ability of politics to respond to rising needs and expectations for governance within and beyond the state may have grown in many instances, though there have also no doubt been cases of decline and regression (e.g. those resulting in state failure). Yet there exists a fundamental mismatch between, on the one hand, the realities of interdependence and rising expectations, and on the other, the capacity for global governance within an effective international order. Significantly, that mismatch is caused by the notion of *sovereignty*, or more precisely by the way that concept is generally

---

2 Robert H. Jackson, *Quasi-States: Sovereignty, International Relations, and the Third World* (Cambridge: Cambridge University Press, 1993).

3 Yuval Noah Harari, *Homo Deus: A Brief History of Tomorrow* (London: Harvill Secker, 2016), 220–77.

understood and practiced. This traditional understanding of sovereignty inhibits the transformation of international politics to within the lines in where it is pushed by the dual dynamics of technological change and the revolution of rising expectations.

Diplomacy finds itself at the edge of this cleavage between the demands of global governance and its supply through national foreign policies: global governance, after all, is nothing but diplomacy or, more precisely, the outcomes of interactions by national diplomacies. As a result of this tension, the outcomes of global governance tend to fall short of what is needed and expected. This lag, in turn, has two different consequences, one direct, one indirect. The direct consequence concerns what we discussed above – the lag between the demands of international governance and the existing arrangements by international cooperation. Yet the capacity for global governance may also be affected by the transformation of national politics through its impact on states' capacity and willingness to engage in international cooperation.[4] The corrosive impact of this tension by now seems to have affected a number of Western liberal democracies. However, it has also been evident in autocracies, for example in the People's Republic of China. There, the Communist Party recognized the danger of its policies being insufficient to cope with the enormous challenges of China's transformation. It is currently trying to respond by installing a system of governance that concentrates power at the top in an effort to speed up and effectuate China's governance in line with the requirements of technological change and rising expectations, and making the fullest possible use of information and communication technology advances. If successful, the 'Chinese model' of technocratic authoritarian governance may well become the yardstick against which the performance of other models will be measured.

The Concept of Foreign Policy Autism

A victim of this corrosion of national politics by tensions between the demand for and supply of (global) governance has been foreign policy, in what might be described as autistic tendencies in national politics. The term "autism" was originally coined by the Swiss psychiatrist Eugen Bleuler in 1911 to describe a form of unsocial behaviour by individuals.

4 Francis Fukuyama, *Political Order and Political Decay: From the Industrial Revolution to the Globalization of Democracy* (New York: Profile Books, 2014).

For him, autism was a crucial symptom of schizophrenia: a withdrawal from the outside world into one's own, internal world. Sigmund Freud took up the concept and similarly used it to denote certain behavioural anomalies in his patients.

The concept has occasionally been used as a metaphor in International Relations (IR) theory.[5] There, it is based on the analogy drawn between the behaviour of individuals and that of states – an analogy not without problems, but still used frequently in IR theory.[6] I am aware of only two reasonably systematic efforts to apply the metaphor of autism as developed by Bleuler and Freud to the analysis of foreign policy and international relations. The more extensive of the two efforts was undertaken by *Karl W. Deutsch* and his German protégé *Dieter Senghaas*. In a co-authored article, they used Freud's psychoanalytical terminology to analyse, in general terms, foreign policy behaviour.[7] Senghaas took this analogy further in his work on nuclear deterrence and "threat policy" in the context of the Cold War; in his work, the concept of autism assumed a key role. According to Deutsch and Senghaas, governments can be compared to an individual's ego that constantly struggles to reconcile contradictory demands and pressures from within and without. Within the individual, the demands are made by the "id", along with its own, emotional and instinct-driven inclinations towards the immediate gratification of desires, and the "superego", representing internalized parental and societal demands. These inner demands have to be reconciled by the ego with the demands of the "reality principle" – that is, with the constraints and opportunities in the individual's real external environment. Senghaas saw deterrence and threat policies as autistic: the governments that pursued such policies, he argued, constructed their own, distorted perceptional images of the reality of international relations that surrounded them, and then legitimated their actions and their results (for example, responses by the "adversary") in terms of

5 Stephen Michael Christian, "Autism in International Relations: A Critical Assessment of International Relations' Autism Metaphors", *European Journal of International Relations* 24, no. 2 (June 2018; first published March 2017): 464–88.

6 The critique of the metaphor's use as developed by Christian, accusing it of involving a form of "ableism", seems beside the point, given this analogy: while the desire to protect individuals from being regarded as 'unsocial' and therefore in some way ill seems well-intentioned and understandable (though not necessarily persuasive), its application by analogy to states logically falls into an entirely different context.

7 Karl W. Deutsch and Dieter Senghaas, "Die brüchige Vernunft von Staaten", in *Kritische Friedensforschung*, ed. Dieter Senghaas, 6th ed. (Frankfurt, 1981), 105–63.

those perceptions as conclusive evidence that justified the initial decisions and encouraged policies that doubled down on those decisions.[8]

Edward Luttwak is the other author who has used the concept of autism. In his book *The Rise of China versus the Logic of Strategy*[9] he developed the theory that China has been unable to develop and execute a grand strategy because it held a grossly simplified and misleading view of reality. Luttwak attributes this "strategic autism" to the fact that China had been cut off from the rest of the world beyond East Asia for most of its history. According to Luttwak, China attributes to the U.S. motives and objectives (such as the urge to expand and dominate others) it would hold itself if it were in America's position, and it is unable to look at the world in any other way than through an exclusively Chinese lens. As a result, China simplifies reality into very schematic representations, leading it to fall into opportunism and gamesmanship.

How accurate and useful Senghaas' views on nuclear deterrence during the Cold War or Luttwak's take on China's grand strategy are is debatable, but this does not need to concern us here. I am interested in the broader argument that both are making: under certain circumstances, states – like individuals – may be seriously hampered in their ability to perceive and respond to their international environment adequately, a policy deficiency they label autism. I suggest this concept is useful to describe (as in fact does the contemporary understanding of autism in psychology) a *spectrum* of problematic foreign policy behaviour patterns by states. For these purposes, I define *foreign policy autism* (FPA) as follows:

a) FPA describes patterns of foreign policy behaviour that are persistently inappropriate (i.e., either too ineffective or too disruptive to realize the enlightened collective interests of the state and its people).
b) FPA can result from specific political dysfunctions or from emotionally charged politics.
c) As an expression of political dysfunctions, FPA may result from excessive involvement of organized interests in foreign policy decision-making. As Mancur Olson has persuasively argued in his *The Rise and Decli-*

8 Dieter Senghaas, "Towards an Analysis of Threat Policy" (1974), in Dieter Senghaas, *Pioneer of Peace and Development Research*, Springer Briefs on Pioneers in Science and Practice, 6 (Heidelberg: Springer, 2013), 27–71.

9 Edward N. Luttwak, *The Rise of China vs. the Logic of Strategy*, (Cambridge, MA: Belknap Press of Harvard University Press, 2012), 12ff.

ne of Nations,[10] societies that are economically and socially successful over long periods of time will tend to suffer a proliferation of vested interests that will slow down and constrain policy-making towards lowest common denominators and short-termism. Another dysfunctional aspect of politics may be excessive tactical use of foreign policy decisions in domestic political manoeuvres. (The qualifier 'excessive' is important here: it implies that those weaknesses are 'normal' if they remain within reasonable limits, but 'problematic' if they become dominant in foreign policy behaviour).

d) FPA as 'emotional politics' results from images and perceptions of the world that are grossly distorted through emotionally charged collective attitudes – feelings such as fear, loathing and a hatred of 'enemies', guilt over past events, or envy and frustration over one's own current status. As Senghaas and others have shown, such dysfunctional perceptions of world politics tend towards auto-immunization. They become 'closed', that is, resistant to contradictory observations. The resulting 'theory' or perceptional 'model' of the world is able to explain any observation whatsoever in ways that support the model. Thus, if Beijing is persuaded that it is America's intention to block China's rise, any American policy and decision will be seen as a stratagem arising from that nefarious U.S. desire.

Freud defined the "id" as a part of the mind, and he observed that

> "cut off from the external world [the id] has a world of perception of its own. It detects with extraordinary acuteness certain changes in its interior, especially oscillations in the tension of its instinctual needs, and these changes become conscious as feelings in the pleasure-unpleasure series. [...] Self-perceptions [...] govern the passage of events in the id with despotic force. The id obeys the inexorable pleasure principle."[11]

In our analogy, 'instincts' would be organized interests, but also collective emotions, such as nationalist fervour. Again, it should be pointed out that we are talking here about patterns of behaviour that are 'normal' in princi-

10 Mancur Olson, *The Rise and Decline of Nations: Economic Growth, Stagflation, and Social Rigidities* (New Haven, CT: Yale University Press, 1982).

11 Sigmund Freud, "The Unconscious" (1940), 198, quoted in *The Unconscious: A Bridge between Psychoanalysis and Cognitive Neuroscience*, ed. Marianne Leuzinger-Bohleber, Simon Arnold and Mark Solms (Abingdon and New York: Routledge, 2017).

ple: any foreign policy will reflect organized societal interests to some degree, and will depend on a modicum of emotional commitment, not only on reasoned support. Thus there is a fine line, or perhaps even a grey area, dividing 'healthy' or 'normal' from 'autistic' foreign policies. Nevertheless, to highlight the difference when evaluating national foreign policy performances is meaningful – and important.

There are several reasons why present circumstances may be favouring FPA in both its variants: *ineffectiveness* and *disruptive behaviour* ('lashing out'). *FPA as ineffectiveness* could be expected to result from decades of increasing wealth and high levels of social stability that much of the Western world has experienced since the 1950s. There can be no doubt that this has produced a proliferation of organized material and ideational interests along the lines of Mancur Olson's theory of growth and decline. This trend has been mirrored also at the level of party systems. The number of parties represented in parliaments has tended to increase over the last decades, making the formation of government with stable majorities and clear policy profiles more difficult.[12] As globalization has intruded ever more deeply into economies and societies, the boundaries between domestic and foreign affairs, and hence between domestic and transnational interests, have become continually more blurred, aggravating the tendencies for foreign policy to be drawn into the domestic political arena. Finally, the proliferation of interests and the transnationalisation of economies and societies through globalization have, of course, been multidimensional and contradictory: there are interests that favour globalization because they benefit, and those that oppose it, because they lose. Yet as these crisscrossing tendencies and forces compete with each other in efforts to shape policy decisions, the net result will often be to make the issues more complex and intractable, and the design and implementation of 'good' foreign policies therefore objectively more complicated and demanding.

Not all of these factors will necessarily strengthen autistic tendencies in foreign policy-making, and some may well even work against them. The connectivities between societies that globalization encourages, for example, may undermine the tendencies towards closure of perceptions. Yet on balance there are still convincing reasons to worry about the capacity of the foreign policy process to produce, and of governments to implement,

12 Majority voting systems, such as those in America, Britain and France, have to some extent been formally immune to those tendencies, but political positions beyond the major parties, supported by many voters, have also thereby led to an erosion of the old party systems.

policies that are effective in meeting the demands for global governance. The problems will first surface in individual decisions, but as the negative tendencies of gridlock gain momentum, such decisions could become more frequent and begin to affect basic foreign policy orientations.

Disruptive FPA could take the form of a political lashing-out of the kind we presently observe in the foreign policy decisions and actions of U.S. President Donald Trump, or that we saw earlier in the result of the referendum on Brexit in the UK. Disruptive FPA ultimately reflects the divisive, corrosive impact of globalization on (Western) societies. For the last quarter of a century, the dominant narrative of prosperity and social stability has only told part of the story. Far-reaching changes in work and employment patterns have produced pervasive stress, increasing social inequalities, and closed-off horizons for significant parts of our societies, including sections of the middle classes that have found themselves under downward pressure. The continuing strength of nationalism and the rise of populism across the Western world point to the strong, increasing 'oscillations in the tension' within our societies.

As in its original field of psychology, the concept of FPA does not pretend to explain; it offers a dense, analytically focused way of describing behaviour. The possible value-added of this metaphor lies in identifying behavioural patterns, in this case patterns in national foreign policy behaviour, as 'deviant' or 'dysfunctional'. Moreover, the FPA metaphor can identify weaknesses in foreign policy decision-making (such as the misrepresentation of the external environment in a foreign policy or its emotional baggage), and suggest ways to address them. Authoritarian polities might be more prone to (emotionally charged) disruptive FPA, while democracies can be expected to be more susceptible to the ineffectiveness type of FPA. Yet the United States under Trump and Britain after the Brexit referendum are but two examples of the former type of FPA existing in seemingly consolidated Western democracies; on the other hand, authoritarian political systems can also fall prey to ineffectiveness FPA as a result of gridlock or the dominance of interest groups that block effective foreign policies.

FPA and the European Union

European integration may well illustrate what might happen with international order, and hence with international diplomacy, in the future. The European Union (EU) represents a political space within which interdependence has assumed a density that makes it comparable to interdependence within societies; it attempts to organize this space politically on the basis of a new concept of sovereignty – 'shared sovereignty'.[13] Unfortunately, in recent years the EU reinforces a sceptical perspective on governance beyond the nation state. Within the EU, the heightened pressure on politics seems to have resulted in a shift of attention by governments towards domestic politics and towards short-term expedience – in other words, towards 'autism'. In fact, FPA seems to have been at work at two levels within the EU: at the member-state level and at that of the EU's Common Foreign and Security Policy (CFSP).

Effective governance of the EU will be impossible without an approach to politics that gives space to mutual empathy, a willingness to compromise and accommodate other interests, and a conceptual framework (e.g., an understanding of sovereignty) that is compatible with these requirements. Under the conditions of democratic politics, this needs polities that are solidly behind by a basic pro-European consensus and a commitment to democratic *alternance* only within the parameters of this consensus. To survive and prosper, the EU may therefore be dependent not only on effective national governance but also on a certain kind of national polity – one with robust public support for concepts of national identity, sovereignty and politics that are compatible with policies which can effectively promote the enlightened self-interest of the EU's peoples, individually and collectively. To that end, political choices, sometimes bold ones, will need to be made against a backdrop of uncertainty and unpredictability. They cannot be expected only to provide benefits, but will also involve costs that need to be shared and risks that need to be carried collectively. Yet it is far from clear whether such robust political support for enlightened policies (and hence for effective diplomacy) exists in all present member states – indeed, in *any* member state!

To the extent that the national foundations for European politics have become problematic, European diplomacy has already encountered significant difficulties in realizing the common good, or indeed even the enlightened national self-interest of individual member states. For example, has it really been in Germany's enlightened national interest to impose its own kind of adjustment on Greek society in the Euro crisis? Overall, the constraints on national foreign policies imposed by prevalent concepts of

---

13 See Anthony Barnett, "Why Brexit Won't Work: The EU is about Regulation Not Sovereignty", *Open Democracy UK*, 25 June 2018, https://www.opendemocracy.net/anthony-barnett/why-brexit-won-t-work-eu-is-about-regulation-not-sovereignty (accessed 23 July 2018).

sovereignty concerning common policies in recent years have produced a series of crises in the EU that, taken together, threaten its future viability, perhaps even its existence "as we know it."[14] At the core of this problem lie deficiencies within and deep ideological and identity differences between the polities that make up the EU. Recently the differences have been exacerbated by migration pressure.[15] Those crises reflect the tensions that have accumulated between the forces of globalization and rising expectations, on the one hand, and Europe's collective political efforts to channel and domesticate them, on the other. The latter bear the hallmarks of FPA in both its forms: inefficiency and emotional bias. While the nature of the crises may demand major change, it is not clear whether the decision-making capacities of the EU are capable of such change. Incrementalism on a downward slope towards minimalist policy adjustments seems much more likely. A similar picture emerges if we consider CFSP: the EU's ability to hold its own as a powerful and influential player, and its performance in world politics as a paragon of international order leaves (to put it mildly) a lot to be desired.

This troubling story of European integration over the last decade may well offer a glimpse into the future of world politics, which faces a comparable conundrum (though on a much larger scale) of rapidly deepening (if uneven) interdependence, integration and rising expectations set against insufficiently responsive governance at the national and (even more so) at the international level. What supports this sceptical prognosis is that not only the EU, but many other international organizations find themselves in crisis, starting with the United Nations. International politics seems to display problems similar to those at the national level of politics. Its responses to changing material circumstances due to technological advances and to rising expectations and demands appear to be lagging behind, often with a widening gap. Diplomacy may therefore find itself more and more constrained in its scope and in its ability to promote change through arguments because of problems rooted in FPA.

One way in which politics at the national level has tried to respond to the challenges of the age is to amass more power at the top of the hierarchy. Yet superior national power is unlikely to bridge the gap and compensate for the lag, for several reasons. First, the autistic qualities of national

---

14 Olivier Bouin, "The End of European Integration as We Know It", in *Europe's Crises*, ed. Manuel Castells et al. (Cambridge, UK, Medford, MA: Polity, 2017); John R. Gillingham, *The EU: An Obituary* (London and New York: Verso, 2016).

15 Ivan Krastev, *After Europe* (Philadelphia, PA: University of Pennsylvania Press, 2017).

politics and policies work against the kind of effective international cooperation that would be needed to mobilize sufficient power resources. Second, FPA would work against accommodating external demands through effective internal adjustments, but instead look for easy alternatives by deflecting the burden or ignoring the problem. Third, faced with such difficulties, international cooperation may opt for face-saving pseudo-solutions and compromise formulas that fall far short of what is necessary.

Future Implications

What are the implications of this analysis for diplomacy in the 21st century – or, more modestly, over the next two decades? If the challenge to diplomacy in this new age of globalization is the sustainable and peaceful resolution of conflicts about who gets what between countries through reasoning and mutual adjustment guided by enlightened self-interest, then it seems likely to be squeezed badly by the contradictory trends of, on the one hand, rising demands on global governance rooted in deepening interdependence, and on the other, the increasing assertion of individual and narrow collective interests that seem to be a catalyst for FPA.

Of course, this definition of diplomacy does not exhaust the broad variety of functions that diplomacy serves and diplomats carry out. States will continue to exist, and probably continue to play the principal role in international politics. Their governments will carry on interacting with each other through diplomacy. There will no doubt also continue to be circumstances in which the domestic context will not constrain or even derail prudent and effective foreign policy decisions. While the scope for diplomacy in its essential functions may indeed be squeezed by FPA, diplomacy and diplomats will continue to operate within the remaining political space, and a key element will continue to be the forging of coalitions.[16] Yet diplomacy can also expect to be instrumentalised as interpreter and megaphone for national concerns and engage in posturing, while its role as a constituency of empathy for others and for reasoned compromise will likely suffer. This, in turn, would affect the recruitment of diplomats and their profes-

16 Sophie Eisentraut, *Coalition Building and Compromise Are the Future of Global Leadership. Here's Why*, German Marshall Fund, 18 September 2017, htttps://outoforder.gmfus.org/coalition-building-and-compromise-are-the-future-of-global-leadership-heres-why-4d34b2d353dd (accessed 20 September 2017).

sional ethics. Will it be '*right or wrong, my government?*' or will it be '*helping to put my country on a good track?*'

From the perspective of our autism metaphor, we would expect 'well-governed' states in this context of global governance to behave in ways comparable to how a 'mature' individual would behave. Thus, they would exhibit a capacity to manage the conflicting pressures from within and from the outside world in ways allowing them to optimize their enlightened national self-interests by interacting responsibly and empathically with others. Good diplomacy requires carefully collected, thoroughly analysed assessments of the world, both in terms of the particular external environment in which a specific foreign policy decision, or a policy or a strategy are to unfold, and of the stakes involved for its own society and polity. Its decisions, policies and strategies need to be emotionally mature and sensitive to biases that might distort decisions and render them ineffective or, worse, dangerous. Its implementation requires empathy and persuasive skills. This is what the world will need from its diplomats. Whether outdated notions of sovereignty and tendencies towards FPA will allow them to do their job well depends on the capacity of states, and specifically of European and Western democracies, to take corrective action to re-define their own roles in global governance and to overcome those worrying tendencies.

Digital Diplomacy as Diplomatic Sites: Emotion, Identity & Do-it-Yourself Politics

R. S. Zaharna

Even as digital diplomacy takes the diplomatic community by storm, we are still only in the early stages of appreciating the broader impact of digital and social media on diplomacy. To date, 'digital diplomacy' appears to be an extension of traditional, state-centric diplomacy. New media emerge as new tools for meeting state goals and interests. The immediate challenge becomes how to master these tools before – or better than – rival state and non-state actors.

This view of digital diplomacy as a diplomatic tool satisfies only a first-level analysis. The second-level analysis involves apprehending those ways in which the media are fostering new diplomatic spaces. These diplomatic spaces are animated by public participation, expectations, and needs, including profound identity needs. The public dynamics of these spaces may challenge traditional mores of state-centric diplomacy. Nevertheless, mastering the dynamics of these spaces is critical.

State-Centric Digital Diplomacy: Digital Media as Diplomatic Tools

For the rational, pragmatic state actor, digital and social media accord unprecedented global reach and enticing potential for diplomatic innovation. Recent digital diplomacy reports by private and government researchers highlight the obstacles and opportunities regarding digital media for diplomacy and foreign ministries.[1]

Digital diplomacy has become increasingly reliant on innovations in strategic communication. Strategic communication is the gold standard for

1 Australian Government, Department of Foreign Affairs and Trade, *Digital Media Strategy 2016–18* (Barton, November 2016), http://dfat.gov.au/about-us/publications/corporate/Documents/digital-media-strategy-2016-18.pdf (accessed 20 March 2018); Shaun Rioardan, *The Strategic Use of Digital and Public Diplomacy in Pursuit of National Objectives* (Barcelona: Federació d'Organitzacions Catalanes Internacionalment Reconegudes [FOCIR], 2016).

designing persuasive messages and media strategies for enhancing national images, advocating policies, and influencing publics. Strategic communication is instrumental in the competitive pursuit among countries to enhance their soft power.[2] Although Nye speaks of soft power as "intangible", the ability to "wield" soft power resources is established through communication. As Rawnsley has remarked, "If no one knows about one's values and good deeds, where's the power?"[3]

Digital diplomacy's reach and efficiency is increasingly amplified by networking approaches. Networking strategies can enhance the circulation of information, collaboration with others, and engagement opportunities with publics. Networking can transform static messages into more dynamic strategic narratives.[4] While states are keen to master new digital tools, so are other political actors. Digital media have empowered non-state political actors capable of rivalling state communication efforts. Digital media have brought state and non-state actors into reciprocal contact with the very same publics that they are trying to influence.

Mixed Results

Scholars have seen a significant spike in the number of states deploying digital media and strategic communication to join the soft power competition. However, what they are not seeing is significant gains, such as increased favourability ratings by foreign publics, to match these increased efforts and investments. The results appear mixed.

Surprisingly perhaps, aggressive strategic communication may aggravate rather than enhance global relations. Nye posited that the pursuit of soft power would improve relations. Researchers now question that assumption, citing the competition for soft power among Asian countries as a driver of greater friction than friendship.[5]

2 Jonathan McClory (USC Center on Public Diplomacy), *The Soft Power 30: A Global Ranking of Soft Power 2017* (Portland Group/USC Center on Public Diplomacy, July 2017), http://softpower30.com/wp-content/uploads/2017/07/The-Soft-Power-30-Report-2017-Web-1.pdf (accessed 20 March 2018).

3 Gary Rawnsley, "Approaches to Soft Power and Public Diplomacy in China and Taiwan", *The Journal of International Communication* 18, no. 2 (2012): 121–35 (123).

4 Alister Miskimmon, Ben O'Loughlin and Laura Roselle, *Strategic Narratives: Communication Power and the New World Order* (New York: Routledge, 2013).

5 Ian Hall and Frank Smith, "The Struggle for Soft Power in Asia: Public Diplomacy and Regional Competition", *Asian Security* 9, no. 1 (January 2013): 1–18; Jan Melissen and Yul Sohn, *Leveraging Middle Power Public Diplomacy in East Asian Internatio-*

Strategic communication appears less precise with diverse, global publics. Perhaps nowhere has strategic communication been more urgently pursued than in efforts to counter violent extremism (CVE). While there have been intensive studies to develop counter-narrative strategies, their use has often produced counter-intuitive outcomes.[6] Rather than winning hearts and minds in the Islamic world, new groups such as the "Islamic State" (ISIS) have been successful in recruiting youth in Western societies. Furthermore, these groups were often able to use counter-narratives for their purposes of radicalizing and recruiting.

The rising tide of populism represents another critical concern for the use of strategic communication in diplomacy. The focus of strategic communication on persuasion may actually undermine inter-group mediation efforts. Research suggests that the intent to influence can be met with greater resistance as attitudes are hardened rather than changed. The result is polarization. The *2017 Global Risks Report* by the World Economic Forum warned of "deepening social and cultural polarization", as a threat that could undermine democracy.[7]

Public-Centric Digital Diplomacy: Digital Media and Diplomatic Sites

Conspicuously overlooked in analyses of the power dynamics between states and even non-state actors in digital diplomacy is the participation of *publics* in the diplomatic equation. From a public perspective, digital media appear to represent a new diplomatic space for public participation and expression. When publics speak of "going online", they are suggesting a place. The online environment represents a place for people to meet and interact.

---

nal Relations, Issue Briefing (Seoul: The East Asia Institute, 24 November 2015), http://www.eai.or.kr/data/bbs/eng_report/2015112410453330.pdf (accessed 4 September 2017).

6 Cristina Archetti, "Terrorism, Communication and New Media: Explaining Radicalization in a Digital Age", *Perspectives on Terrorism* 9, no. 1 (2015): 49–59; Bibi T. van Ginkel, *Responding to Cyber Jihad: Towards an Effective Counter-Narrative*, ICCT Research Paper (The Hague: The International Centre for Counter-Terrorism, March 2015), https://www.icct.nl/download/file/ICCT-van-Ginkel-Responding-To-Cyber-Jihad-Towards-An-Effective-Counter-Narrative-March2015.pdf (accessed 20 March 2018).

7 World Economic Forum, *The Global Risks Report 2017*, 12th ed. (Geneva, 2017), 58, http://www3.weforum.org/docs/GRR17_Report_web.pdf (accessed 20 March 2018).

Awareness of these new public spaces and its implications for diplomacy appears to have grown gradually. Several scholars have suggested that diplomacy is becoming "more public" – not necessarily in terms of *the audience* (i.e., diplomacy directed at the public), but rather *the context* (i.e., diplomacy conducted in the public arena). Hockings and his colleagues suggested the term "integrative diplomacy" to capture the complexity of the public stage that diplomats must now share with a broad range of actors.[8] Gregory recommended adding a "public dimension" to diplomacy.[9] Kelley has perhaps been the most forceful, stating that "diplomacy is well beyond the point of opening itself to the public – it is becoming enmeshed within the public domain."[10]

The new diplomatic space is not defined by its actors – whether state, non-state or publics – so much as by its communication dynamics. In this regard, these diplomatic spaces might be more accurately captured by Neumann's term "diplomatic sites", which place diplomacy in the realm of social reality.[11] The online dynamics, while virtual in theory, can be very real to the participants – and have actual consequences for diplomats. Phenomena such as Brexit, Trump, and anti-immigrant sentiment are part of those consequences. Therefore it is critical for diplomats to understand the dynamics of these new diplomatic sites.

Emotion as a Defining Dynamic

Emotion has become a defining dynamic of these new diplomatic sites. Emotions permeate nearly every aspect of the online experience, from the hand-held nature of the electronic devices, to the immediacy of real-time

---

8 Brian Hocking, Jan Melissen, Shaun Riordan and Paul Sharp, *Futures for Diplomacy: Integrative Diplomacy in the 21st Century*, Report No. 1 (The Hague: Netherlands Institute of International Relations 'Clingendael', October 2012), https://www.clingendael.nl/publication/futures-diplomacy-integrative-diplomacy-21st-century (accessed 20 March 2018).

9 Bruce Gregory, *The Paradox of Public Diplomacy: Its Rise and 'Demise'* (Washington, D.C.: Institute of Public Diplomacy and Global Communication, February 2014).

10 John Robert Kelley, "The New Diplomacy: Evolution of a Revolution", *Diplomacy & Statecraft* 21, no. 2 (June 2010): 286–305.

11 Iver B. Neumann, *Diplomatic Sites: A Critical Enquiry* (New York: Oxford University Press, 2013).

personal interaction, to visuals that sear our sensibilities.[12] Alongside YouTube videos of cute cats are beheadings posted by extremists. Diplomats can expect this dynamic to intensify as technical innovations alter sensory experiences. The popularity of virtual and augmented reality gaming, for example, rests in part upon immersive media technologies that heighten emotional involvement.

While emotion may be implicit in traditional diplomacy, in the public space it is likely to be more explicit, even deliberately vocal, visible and disruptive. Innovations in diplomacy will require heightened sensitivity to develop not just effective, but *affective* strategies that respond to the emotions of the public.

Personalized Do-it Yourself Politics

In these new diplomatic sites, emotion and political action coalesce to become personalized. Established or recognizable political actors are joined by the rising phenomenon of spontaneous personal networks. Bennett called the rise of "large-scale, rapidly forming political participation" and "personalized politics" one of the most notable trends in the first decade of the 21st century.[13] He labelled the phenomenon "Do-it-yourself" politics. Danah Boyd termed it "me and my gang."[14] She pointed to a shift in publics forming around topical issues towards personal networks.

While marketing and technology are fuelling a more personalized online experience, the drive toward personalized politics can pose critical challenges for diplomacy. Personalized self-defined politics can undermine larger social institutions and protocols that maintain social cohesion. This

12 Tovah Benski and Eran Fisher, eds., *The Internet and Emotions*, Routledge Studies in Science, Technology and Society, 22 (New York: Routledge, 2014); Javier Serrano-Puche, *Emotions and Digital Technologies: Mapping the Field of Research in Media Studies*, MEDIA@LSE Working Papers 33 (London: London School of Economics and Political Science, 2015), http://www.lse.ac.uk/media@lse/research/mediaWorking Papers/pdf/WP33-FINAL.pdf (accessed 20 March 2018).

13 W. Lance Bennett, "The Personalization of Politics: Political Identity, Social Media, and Changing Patterns of Participation", *The Annals of the American Academy of Political and Social Science* 644, no. 1 (November 2012): 20–39.

14 Danah Boyd, "Can Social Network Sites Enable Political Action?", in *Rebooting America*, ed. Allison H. Fine, Micah L. Sifry, Andrew Rasiej and Josh Levy (San Francisco, CA: Personal Democracy Press, 2008), 112–16.

is the point of "disruptive power"[15] and the tactics of the "outrage industry."[16] Recent breaches of diplomatic protocol are repercussions of this emerging dynamic.

Story-Driven Resonant Narratives

If one looks closely at the political discourse of personal politics, people are not just sharing information. They are sharing stories. While the Arab Spring was initially heralded as a social media revolution, researchers now credit the story-driven nature of the phenomenon.[17] These stories are not carefully crafted strategic narratives but emotionally resonant narratives of affinity and identity.

The combination of personal tools and personal stories – or emotional media with emotional messages – can create a diplomatic space that is hyper-emotional. Emotionally powerful stories can even override hard facts. Online anger can become offline outrage. Noted sociologist Manuel Castells in *Networks of Outrage and Hope* found that fear and hope repeatedly surface as the two most salient emotions in creating what he called "emotional movements."[18] When publics confront officials as an emotional movement, an immediate empathic response is often critical to successfully mediate and deescalate tensions, according to emerging crisis research.[19]

Emotion and Identity

Next to emotion, identity emerges as a strong undercurrent in these diplomatic spaces. In much the same way that states appear driven to enhance and promote a positive national image, publics appear driven by profound

---

15 Taylor Owen, *Disruptive Power: The Crisis of the State in the Digital Age* (Oxford: Oxford University Press, 2015).

16 Jeffrey M. Berry and Sarah Sobeiraj, *The Outrage Industry: Political Opinion Media and the New Incivility* (Oxford: Oxford University Press, 2014).

17 Zizi Papacharissi, *Affective Publics: Sentiment, Technology, and Politics* (Oxford: Oxford University Press, 2015).

18 Manuel Castells, *Networks of Outrage and Hope: Social Movements in the Internet Age* (Cambridge: Polity, 2012).

19 Matthew W. Seeger, "Best Practices in Crisis Communication", *Journal of Applied Communication Research* 34, no. 3 (August 2006): 232–44.

identity needs. Identity is not only about self-expression; it is also about self-validation, especially in turbulent or uncertain times.

In the online environment, identity can be a shared feeling. People recognize themselves in the emotions of others: "angry like me." Vigilant diplomats will note that when identity is linked to emotions, publics can become fluid, changing entities. Fixed labels for political actors and publics, such as demographics (age, income), geography (domestic/foreign, or Europe/Mideast) or socio-cultural groups (youth, Muslim) may not be as helpful as they once were. More disconcerting still, fluid identity boundaries can occur between national boundaries and, increasingly, within national boundaries. An incident among domestic publics or with the government can go viral, with global implications.[20]

Emotion and Community

Publics are not just identifying with others through emotion. Shared emotions also can create community. In contrast to scholars who use the term "network" to study people using social media, the people actually using these tools speak of "community."[21] Emotions are the glue that can transform a network of individual nodes with relational ties into a community with powerful social bonds.

Online virtual communities sustained by emotional connections and a sense of belonging can have real consequences as members seek each other offline to promote their agenda. For example, despite the group's lethal agenda, ISIS recruitment exemplifies a highly relational and emotional approach that stresses shared identity and belonging. Their call to the *Ummah* is relational, speaking to ties of a brotherhood of Muslims. Emotional *perspective taking and empathy* are also pivotal recruitment tools. Researchers have noted how ISIS recruiters seek to "engage individuals as individuals [...] interlocutors listen and respond to their personal concerns and the details of their lives, making them feel valued and cared for and creating a

20 R. S. Zaharna and Nur Uysal, "Going for the Jugular in Public Diplomacy: How Adversarial Publics Using Social Media Are Challenging State Legitimacy", *Public Relations Review* 42, no. 1 (March 2016): 109–19.

21 Howard Rheingold, *The Virtual Community: Homesteading on the Electronic Frontier* (MIT Press eBooks, 2000), http://www.rheingold.com/vc/book/ (accessed 20 March 2018).

sense of warmth, inclusion and belonging."[22] Counter-narrative strategies that threaten or demean the community miss the mark in trying to crack the emotional ties that bind the perceived identity within the community.

Implications & Recommendations

The challenge of digital diplomacy is not about digital tools or learning a new medium of communication. The challenge is navigating the dynamics of emerging public diplomatic spaces, which are sprouting online and then flourishing offline. This trend is likely to intensify.

As forces of globalization and digital technologies bring diverse domestic publics together with foreign publics and political actors, diplomacy will need to expand its predominantly state-centric perspective to include a public-centric perspective. Traditionally, diplomats have mediated identities and relations at the state level and from the state perspective. They also did so in a familiar and well-cultivated diplomatic space behind closed doors. The challenge of digital diplomacy will be to innovate in order to effectively monitor and mediate identities within and between publics in today's diplomatic spaces.

Avoiding the State-Centric Strategic Communication Treadmill

In the soft power competition between states, contemporary diplomacy relies heavily – perhaps too heavily – on the tools of influence and digital technologies in order to promote national images, interests, and policies. The illusion of control may keep diplomacy caught on a communication treadmill of creating ever-more sophisticated media and messaging strategies that do little to actually advance diplomatic goals in the new diplomatic space. If digital diplomacy is to achieve in the public domain what traditional diplomacy has achieved behind closed doors, it must move beyond state-centric strategic communication aimed at influence. There may be a much-needed return to diplomacy's forte in mediation and collaboration.

22 Lydia Wilson, "Understanding the Appeal of ISIS", *New England Journal of Public Policy* 29, no. 1 (2017): article 5 (4–5).

Developing an Eye for Public-Centric Needs

Public participation and public needs are part of the diplomatic calculus. Diplomats must develop a public-centric eye for the full range of publics (foreign, domestic, and diaspora), as well as their varying needs for identity, emotion, and participation. "Pragmatic rationalism",[23] which has defined traditional diplomacy among state actors, may be less effective and strategic in meeting public-centric needs and expectations. Diplomatic innovation will mean developing public-centric diplomatic instruments for monitoring emotional dynamics, mediating identities and negotiating conflicts in the public domain.

Leveraging the Human Dimension

As the novelty of the new media becomes old, the thinking of digital diplomacy will be less and less about the digital and more and more about the public. Moving to this second level of analysis paradoxically requires a return to diplomacy's traditional core of managing human relations. It will require developing diplomatic skills for responding to the emotional imperatives of publics, including empathetic response strategies. Pro-active diplomacy initiatives may engage publics around identity issues, bridging the domestic with the global. Ultimately, it is this human dimension that will be the critical leverage point in enhancing diplomacy's effectiveness in tomorrow's online-offline diplomatic spaces.

23 Kelley, "The New Diplomacy" (see note 10), 286–305.

Conclusions – An Open Diplomacy

"The modern art of diplomacy is to use Theodore Roosevelt's big stick, but digitally – and never ever to speak softly"; this or something similar could be a future definition of 21st century 'diplomacy.' Academically, as an intellectual exploration, the Working Group's investigation considered how the upheavals of the international world might affect future diplomacy. Practitioners, on the other hand, want to know what concrete conclusions can be drawn from this exploration. Are there necessarily consequences to be drawn for politics, the work of diplomacy, and or changes to be made to diplomatic instruments? These collected essays by our international group of academics, practitioners, and observers should be followed by at least an attempt at answers to these questions. The ironic redefinition of 'diplomacy' above therefore only exaggerates the obvious signs of changes that might well become requisite. In fact, the working group's final conclusion is rather complex: it is not a checklist for diplomatic reforms, and it is unclear how much will be possible to translate into real-life politics.

*

I. The most profound effect on the actual character of diplomacy of 21st century global changes is that *public spheres* are multiplying in modern states, especially in Western democracies. The fracturing of our societies, a process which is accelerating this century, has given rise to this fragmentation. Our homes, professional worlds, education, interests, experiences, and ideological orientations are increasingly differentiated. Therefore in diplomacy we are engaging with and responding to an increasing variety of actors that span many different and coexisting public spheres. These diverse public spheres exist side by side, sometimes without touching; they can also work together or collide and split into new particles of publics.

This process of pluralization is likely to intensify. It affects a society not only from the inside, but also works inter-societally – that is, cross-border. Consequently, foreign policy developments naturally become topics within the new publics. This is of course the case when foreign policy problems are simultaneously domestic concerns, but it can also happen if a public has an interest in events outside their country's borders. The new publics therefore want to influence the implementation of foreign policy through diplomacy according to their topics of interest. Thus diplomacy no longer only acts purely intergovernmentally for the national goals of a country. Diplomacy must now explain and justify itself domestically and mediate between a state's goals and the public's perspectives. Publics may claim that a government should behave differently from what the political leadership wants; meanwhile, the government claims to represent the interests of the public properly. Even in autocratically ruled states, the disparity between governmental decisions and public values can be observed. These conflicts shatter the confidence of the public in their political leadership, and can tear a society apart.

Diminishing confidence in political leadership can be seen in a positive light. It arises out of the public's desire to participate in national and international decision-making, a trend that came out of the emancipation processes beginning with the Enlightenment. The situation of popular mistrust in politics and its actions – and thus also diplomacy – will likely intensify rather than weaken, and without solving the tension created between the publics and the representatives of a state. First the legitimacy of a government and then that of a state as a whole is in ever greater danger of becoming paler and less effective. This raises the question of whether a state can still act effectively and efficiently. A solution is conceivable, with recourse to that no doubt millennia-old fundamental virtue of diplomacy, as Bismarck (quoted in the introduction) must have had in mind: patient mediation. Yet now this mediation must be performed not only between international partners, but also between state interests and the new publics. This shift will require a renewed understanding of what diplomacy can do, and consensus in a country about the principles of its governance systems. The new publics as well as governments will experience how this works, and, hopefully, process their experiences productively.

II. Digital techniques are establishing themselves as instruments of diplomacy with *dramatic* effects. The process of adapting to new developments that technologies offer is quite advanced in foreign ministries around the world, albeit with great differences across states. *Digital technologies* facilitate communication, accelerate decision-making, multiply the quantity of rapidly available information, and provide social media platforms for communication with the public. The importance of digital connectivity, however, lies not only in technology, which could be compared with, for example, the introduction of the telegraph in the 19th century or the fax machine in the 20th. With the application of technology itself, there comes a shift in the understanding of the very contents of communications. Information is processed using the available technology. The acceleration of communication also makes decision-taking more urgent, which imposes considerable pressure on decision-makers concerning local and national positions. The pressure is magnified by an awareness of competition with other actors. The competition probably has the same technical capabilities but may have different goals. Furthermore, digital media make more facts available, and tend to arrive on the desktop in the exact moment a decision has to be made.

Recent public discussions about Facebook, Twitter, YouTube, etc. have shown that these media are not merely more convenient and far-reaching platforms for dialogue with diplomats' interlocutors. Decisions about the platforms for, frequency of, and publication time of posts are typically made by algorithms rather than humans. An additional concern is that bots and trolls can publish fake 'personal' postings and fake news. Thus, the initiators – whoever they may be – can introduce topics as they please to the diplomatic institution, usually the Ministry of Foreign Affairs and the politicians at its head, and they may present them for public discussions. The emergence of new pathways for public engagement has political consequences and concerns the control of public opinion – and thus also of politics. Digital communication can become propaganda in the broadest sense. Coupled with the demands of new publics for participation and their distance from the state, this may mean that governments are gradually losing the ability to conduct their affairs satisfactorily. Thus the reactions of alert and suspicious publics pose a threat to the legitimacy, effectiveness, and efficiency of governance. Emergent communication technologies can lead to significant changes for the essence of diplomacy by engaging it in the everyday life of a society.

When attempting to solve this problem, digital connectivity must first be understood as 'politics'. Of course, digitization is technology too. The danger of overlooking essential information, for example, can only be avoided or mitigated by carefully thought-out technical processing. More important, however, is the handling of social media and their expected future products. In practical terms, this can mean that governments themselves continue to develop and create algorithms and platforms that meet a government's own requirements. At the same time they must have a philosophy for their application and development, based on the culture and values of a country as well as the purposes of a state.

It makes sense to do this together with other governments, at least within the framework of the EU. Digital connectivity has an international dimension that is more apparent than elsewhere, with strong momentum between EU member states. The new digitization policy, which opens up to new publics, must become the conducting agency of digital processes and their applications.

III. The consequences of increasing social fragmentation within domestic development can also be observed in an international context. The differentiation of trade and traffic between states, the increase in the number of countries with considerable international influence, the loss of order in the international state structure, and doubts about the validity of the rules for liberal international order have clearly recognizable consequences. The most important of these is that the number of *actors* engaging in an international context is increasing. They are, like national actors, different, but also similar to one another; profit- or ideology-oriented, they compete or cooperate with one another. Since they operate internationally, they affect foreign policy and diplomacy directly and sometimes with significant outcomes.

Such outcomes mainly take shape in the more fractured interactions of non-state and state actors. The diversity of actors' interests results in unpredictable processes of interaction. Such processes follow (though less so than in the 20th century) the requirements of international law, that is to say, international regulations – which are themselves less binding, and may even be easily circumvented. Thus, diplomatic interaction pathways intersect with old and new players at different levels. With some – undeniably dramatic – exceptions, there are fewer attempts to seek solutions to problems using the force of arms. Instead, other means of coercion become more important. These are mostly economic and financial in nature and exercise the use of force by non-military means to solve problems that cannot be resolved through negotiation. Given these complex losses in international structures and increasing difficulty in navigating them, there are more and more attempts by state actors to withdraw into their nation-state frameworks.

It is difficult to see how a solution can be found here without an enforcing international authority that is able to direct peaceful international conduct. It would need to be seen as at least as legitimate as a sovereign state, and would have to use traditional or innovative diplomatic means to open up fresh, more open ways of coping with the divisions between the many new and old actors. That is a fundamental task of foreign policy itself. To say that the problem can only be tackled multilaterally, in a time when multilateralism itself is in doubt, gives little cause for confidence. After all, it can be said for Europe that whether it likes it or not, the EU, thanks to its construction, is experimenting with the creation of supra-sovereign institutions of order – which are not to be confused with traditional executive institutions.

IV. The *personality and personal profile* of future diplomats are critically important to the practice of diplomacy in the 21st century. Diplomats will need to represent the fragmentation of their societies, cope socially and linguistically with changing demands, and meet the need for a different approach to publics and to digitization. The selection, training of personnel and career paths must therefore be expanded to meet these new requirements. However, this is a task that the foreign ministries of most countries have long been addressing, albeit with different goals.

*

Among the general considerations of the SWP's Working Group, there was no concluding list of formulas. Ultimately, we can provide only approaches and signposts at a time when questions are becoming more common concerning international politics. After all, we are still at the beginning of our understanding of what the changes in and between the countries of the world really mean to the venerable institution of diplomacy. Old or new diplomacy in the 21st century has the task of working towards its main goal: foreign policy that is conducted by peaceful means. The authors of this volume hope that their reflections will be helpful for the orientation of all who are politically concerned with the redesign of diplomacy.

Selected Bibliography

Adler-Nissen, Rebecca. "Conclusion: Relationalism or Why Diplomats Find International Relations Theory Strange." In *Diplomacy and the Making of World Politics*, edited by Ole Jacob Sending, Vincent Pouliot and Iver B. Neumann, 284–308. Cambridge, MA: Cambridge University Press, 2015.

Aggestam, Karin, and Ann E. Towns, eds. *Gendering Diplomacy and International Negotiation*. Basingstoke: Palgrave Macmillan, 2018.

Baldwin, David A. *Economic Statecraft*. Princeton, NJ: Princeton University Press, 1985.

Bayne, Nicholas, and Stephen Woolcock. "What Is Economic Diplomacy?" In *The New Economic Diplomacy: Decision-Making and Negotiation in International Economic Relations*, edited by Nicholas Bayne and Stephen Woolcock, 1–15, 4th ed. London: Routledge, 2016.

Benski, Tovah, and Eran Fisher, eds.*The Internet and Emotions*. Routledge Studies in Science, Technology and Society, 22. New York: Routledge, 2014.

Berry, David M. *Critical Theory and the Digital*. New York: Bloomsbury, 2014.

Bjola, Corneliu, and Marcus Holmes, eds. *Digital Diplomacy: Theory and Practice*. London: Routledge, 2015.

Blackwill, Robert D., and Jennifer M. Harris. *War by Other Means: Geoeconomics and Statecraft*. Cambridge, MA: The Belknap Press of Harvard University Press, 2016.

Bratton, Benjamin H. *The Stack: On Software and Sovereignty*. Cambridge, MA: MIT Press, 2016.

Castells, Manuel. *Networks of Outrage and Hope: Social Movements in the Internet Age*. Cambridge: Polity, 2012.

Christian, Stephen Michael. "Autism in International Relations: A Critical Assessment of International Relations' Autism Metaphors." In *European Journal of International Relations* 24, no. 2 (June 2018; first published March 2017): 464–88.

Cooper, Andrew F. "The Changing Nature of Diplomacy." In *The Oxford Handbook of Modern Diplomacy*, edited by Andrew Cooper, Jorge Heine and Ramesh Thakur, 35–53. Oxford: Oxford University Press, 2013.

Dany, Charlotte. *Global Governance and NGO Participation: Shaping the Information Society in the United Nations*. London and New York: Routledge, 2013.

Farrow, Ronan. *War on Peace: The End of Diplomacy and the Decline of American Influence*. New York: W. W. Norton & Company, 2018.

Fletcher, Tom. *The Naked Diplomat: Power and Statecraft in the Digital Century*. London: William Collins, 2016.

Fukuyama, Francis. *Political Order and Political Decay: From the Industrial Revolution to the Globalization of Democracy*. New York: Profile Books, 2014.

George, Alexander L. *Forceful Persuasion: Coercive Diplomacy as an Alternative to War.* Washington, D.C.: United States Institute of Peace Press, 1991.

Gilpin, Robert. *The Political Economy of International Relations.* Princeton, NJ: Princeton University Press, 1987.

Gregory, Bruce. *The Paradox of Public Diplomacy: Its Rise and 'Demise'.* Washington, D.C.: Institute of Public Diplomacy and Global Communication, February 2014.

Hamilton, Keith, and Richard Langhorne. *The Practice of Diplomacy: Its Evolution, Theory and Administration.* 2nd ed. London and New York: Routledge, 2011.

Hartley, John, Jean Burgess and Alex Bruns, eds. *A Companion to New Media Dynamics.* Oxford: Wiley-Blackwell, 2013.

Hayden, Craig. *The Rhetoric of Soft Power: Public Diplomacy in Global Contexts.* Lanham, MD: Lexington Books, 2012.

Hill, Christopher. *The National Interest in Question: Foreign Policy in Multicultural Societies.* Oxford: Oxford University Press, 2013.

Hocking, Brian, "Multistakeholder Diplomacy: Forms, Functions, and Frustrations", in *Multistakeholder Diplomacy – Challenges and Opportunities*, ed. Jovan Kurbalija and Valentin Katrandjiev (Geneva: DiploFoundation, 2006), 13–29.

—. "The Ministry of Foreign Affairs and the National Diplomatic System." In *Diplomacy in a Globalizing World: Theories and Practices*, edited by Pauline Kerr and Geoffrey Wiseman, 123–40. New York: Oxford University Press, 2013.

—, and Jan Melissen. *Diplomacy in the Digital Age.* The Hague: Netherlands Institute of International Relations 'Clingendael', July 2015.

—, Jan Melissen, Shaun Riordan and Paul Sharp. *Futures for Diplomacy: Integrative Diplomacy for the 21st Century.* The Hague: Netherlands Institute of International Relations 'Clingendael', 2012. https://www.clingendael.org/sites/default/files/pdfs/20121 030_re search_melissen.pdf (accessed 13 September 2017).

Jackson, Robert H. *Quasi-States: Sovereignty, International Relations, and the Third World.* Cambridge: Cambridge University Press, 1993.

Jakobsen, Peter Viggo. "Coercive Diplomacy." In *The SAGE Handbook of Diplomacy*, ed. Costas M. Constantinou, Pauline Kerr and Paul Sharp, 476–86. London: SAGE, 2016.

Kahler, Miles, ed. *Networked Politics: Agency, Power, and Governance.* Ithaca, NY: Cornell University Press, 2009.

Kitchin, Rob. *The Data Revolution.* Los Angeles, CA: SAGE, 2014.

Koch, Michael. "Wozu noch Diplomaten?" In *Auswärtiges Amt: Diplomatie als Beruf*, edited by Enrico Brandt and Christian Buck, 350–59. Opladen: Leske und Budrich, 2002.

Koops, Joachim A., and Gjovalin Macaj, eds. *The European Union as a Diplomatic Actor.* Basingstoke: Palgrave Macmillan, 2015.

Leira, Halvard. "A Conceptual History of Diplomacy." In *The SAGE Handbook of Diplomacy*, edited by Costas M. Constantinou, Pauline Kerr and Paul Sharp, 28–38. London: SAGE, 2016.

Luttwak, Edward N. “From Geopolitics to Geo-economics: Logic of Conflict, Grammar of Commerce.” *The National Interest* 20 (Summer 1990): 17–23.

McClanahan, Grant V. *Diplomatic Immunity: Principles, Practices, Problems*. London: Hurst, 1989.

Miskimmon, Alister, Ben O’Loughlin, and Laura Roselle. *Strategic Narratives: Communication Power and the New World Order*. New York: Routledge, 2013.

Münkler, Herfried. *Der Wandel des Krieges: Von der Symmetrie zur Asymmetrie*. Weilerswist: Velbrück Wissenschaft, 2006.

Naray, Olivier. “Commercial Diplomacy: An Integrative Framework.” *International Journal of Diplomacy and Economy* 1, no. 2 (2012): 119–33.

Neumann, Iver B. *At Home with the Diplomats: Inside a European Foreign Ministry*. Ithaca and London: Cornell University Press, 2012.

—. *Diplomatic Sites: A Critical Enquiry*. New York: Columbia University Press, 2013.

Okano-Heijmans, Maaike. “Economic Diplomacy.” In *The SAGE Handbook of Diplomacy*, edited by Costas M. Constantinou, Pauline Kerr and Paul Sharp, 552–563. London: SAGE, 2016.

Olson, Mancur. *The Rise and Decline of Nations: Economic Growth, Stagflation, and Social Rigidities*. New Haven, CT: Yale University Press, 1982.

Owen, Taylor. *Disruptive Power: The Crisis of the State in the Digital Age*. Oxford: Oxford University Press, 2015.

Papacharissi, Zizi. *Affective Publics: Sentiment, Technology, and Politics*. Oxford: Oxford University Press, 2015.

Petrov, Petar, Karolina Pomorska and Sophie Vanhoonacker. “The Emerging EU Diplomatic System: Opportunities and Challenges after ‘Lisbon.’” *The Hague Journal of Diplomacy* 7, no. 1 (January 2012): 1–9.

Pigman, Geoffrey Allen. *Contemporary Diplomacy*. Cambridge: Polity Press, 2010.

Riordan, Shaun. *The Strategic Use of Digital and Public Diplomacy in Pursuit of National Objectives*. Barcelona: Federació d’Organitzacions Catalanes Internacionalment Reconegudes (FOCIR), 2016.

Rogers, Richard A. *Information Politics on the Web*. Cambridge, MA: MIT Press, 2004.

Scholte, Jan Aart. “From Government to Governance: Transition to a New Diplomacy.” In *Global Governance and Diplomacy: Worlds Apart?*, edited by Andrew F. Cooper, Brian Hocking and William Maley, 39–60. Basingstoke and New York: Palgrave, 2008.

Seabrooke, Leonard. “Economists and Diplomacy: Professions and the Practice of Economic Policy.” *International Journal* 66, no. 3 (September 2011): 629–42.

Sharp, Paul. *Diplomatic Theory of International Relations*. Cambridge, MA: Cambridge University Press, 2009.

Sizoo, Alexandra and Arne Musch. "City Diplomacy: The Role of Local Governments in Conflict Prevention, Peace-Building and Post-Conflict Reconstruction." In *City Diplomacy*, edited by Arne Musch, Chris van der Valk, Alexandra Sizoo and Kian Tajbakhsh, 7–25. The Hague: VNG International, 2008, http://bibalex.org/baifa/Attachment/Documents/480503.pdf (accessed 25 March 2018).

Slaughter, Anne-Marie. *The Chessboard and the Web – Strategies of Connection in a Networked World*. New Haven, CT, and London: Yale University Press, 2017.

Stuenkel, Oliver. *Post-Western World: How Emerging Powers Are Remaking Global Order*. Malden, MA: Polity Press, 2016.

Stulberg, Adam N. *Well-Oiled Diplomacy: Strategic Manipulation and Russia's Energy Statecraft in Eurasia*. Albany, NY: State University of New York Press, 2007.

Tallberg, Jonas, Thomas Sommerer, Theresa Squatrito and Christer Jönsson. *The Opening Up of International Organizations: Transnational Access in Global Governance*. Cambridge, MA: Cambridge University Press, 2013.

About the Authors

Prof. Dr. Corneliu Bjola

is Associate Professor in Diplomatic Studies at the University of Oxford and Chair of the Oxford Digital Diplomacy Research Group. He is the author or co-editor of six books, including *Countering Online Propaganda and Violent Extremism: The Dark Side of Digital Diplomacy* (2018) and *Digital Diplomacy: Theory and Practice* (2015). His current research interests concern the impact of digital technology on the conduct of diplomacy, with a focus on strategic communication and digital influence as well as on theories and methods for countering digital disinformation and propaganda. @cbjola www.cbjola.com

Prof. Dr. Andrew Cooper

is Professor of Political Science at the University of Waterloo and an Alumni Senior Fellow at the Centre for Global Cooperation Research in Duisburg. His publications include, as author, *The BRICS VSI* (OUP, 2016), *Diplomatic Afterlives* (Polity, 2014) and *Celebrity Diplomacy* (Paradigm, 2007); as co-author, *The G20* (Routledge, 2013), *Intervention without Intervening? OAS and Democracy in the Americas* (Palgrave Macmillan, 2006), and *Relocating Middle Powers* (Melbourne UP: 1993); as editor, *Niche Diplomacy* (Palgrave, 1997); and as co-editor, *The Oxford Handbook of Modern Diplomacy* (OUP, 2013).

Prof. em. Dr. Christer Jönsson

is Professor Emeritus of Political Science at Lund University and a member of the Royal Swedish Academy of Sciences. Diplomacy, international organization, negotiation and transnational relations are among his research interests. His publications include *The Opening Up of International Organizations* (co-author, 2013), *Transnational Actors in Global Governance* (co-editor, 2010) and *Essence of Diplomacy* (co-author 2005), along with several articles in leading academic journals. He is a contributor to the *Routledge Handbook of Diplomacy and Statecraft* (2012) and the *Sage Handbook of Diplomacy* (2016).

Emillie V. de Keulenaar

is a post-graduate research student in New Media and Digital Culture at the University of Amsterdam with an MA in the History of Political Thought and Intellectual History at University College London. She has reviously interned at the Netherlands Institute of International Relations 'Clingendael' and is currently part of OILab, a collective of researchers engaged in examining far-right cultures online. She has written about digital diplomacy in *Global Policy* (2017).

Dr. Sascha Lohmann

is an Associate in the Americas Research Division at SWP. Previously, he was a Fritz Thyssen Fellow at the Weatherhead Center for International Affairs, Harvard University. His research interests include International Relations theory and foreign policy analysis, especially the intersection of political economy and national security in the United States and the European Union, as well as the theory and practice of foreign policy advice and evaluation.

Prof. Dr. Hanns W. Maull

is Senior Distinguished Fellow at SWP and Senior Policy Fellow for China and World Order, and Adjunct Professor of International Relations at the Bologna Center of Johns Hopkins University. Until 2013, he held the Chair for Foreign Policy and International Relations at Trier University. He was also Chairman of the Research Advisory Board and Member of Council at SWP from 2004–2012. He publishes frequently on issues concerning the international order, Eastern Asia and European foreign and security policy.

Prof. Dr. Jan Melissen

is Senior Research Fellow at the Netherlands Institute of International Relations 'Clingendael', a Senior Fellow at the Institute of Security and Global Affairs at Leiden University, The Hague Campus, and Professor of Diplomacy at the University of Antwerp. He is a non-resident Faculty Fellow at the Center on Public Diplomacy, University of Southern California, Los Angeles, and Senior Fellow with the Charhar Institute in Beijing. Jan Melissen is founding Co-Editor of The Hague Journal of Diplomacy and Editor of the Diplomatic Studies book series with Brill|Nijhoff.

Kim B. Olsen

is an advisor to the Danish Foreign Ministry and a PhD Fellow at the University of Antwerp. His research interests include German, French, and

European foreign policy and geoeconomic diplomacy. In addition to his current role as the Danish stabilisation advisor to the Syrian conflict, he has previously worked as foreign policy advisor to the Danish embassies in Berlin and Paris, and as a research assistant at the Center for German and European Studies, UC Berkeley.

Dr. Volker Stanzel

is a retired German diplomat who served as Political Director and Ambassador to Japan and China. Since 2015, he is Senior Distinguished Fellow at the SWP in Berlin and heads the project "Diplomacy in the 21st century"; in 2018 he became Vice President of the German Council of Foreign Relations (DGAP). Since 2014 he has taught IR at Claremont McKenna College, the University of California Santa Cruz, Free University Berlin and Dokkyo University in Japan, and now teaches at Hertie School of Governance in Berlin. He holds a Ph.D. in Japanese Studies, Sinology and Political Science from Cologne University, and publishes frequently on East Asian and on various other political topics.

Karsten D. Voigt

is a member of the board of Aspen Germany, and Senior Associate Fellow and Member of the Presidium of the German Council on Foreign Policy. From 1976–1998 he was a member of the German Bundestag. There he served as the Foreign Policy Speaker of the Social Democratic Fraction from 1983–1998. For many years he was chairman of the German-Soviet and later the German-Russian parliamentary group. From 1992–94 he was elected Vice-president and from 1994–96 as President of the Parliamentary Assembly of NATO. From 1999–2010 he served as the German-American Coordinator in the Federal Foreign Office.

Prof. Dr. R. S. Zaharna

is Director of the Global Media program in the School of Communication at the American University in Washington, D.C., and faculty fellow at the Center on Public Diplomacy at the University of Southern California. Her publications include among others *Relational, Networked and Collaborative Approaches to Public Diplomacy* (Routledge, 2013, with A. Arsenault and A. Fisher) and *Battles to Bridges: U.S. Strategic Communication and Public Diplomacy after 9/11* (Palgrave MacMillan, 2010). She is currently working on her new book, *Globalizing Public Diplomacy: Communication in a Digitally Connected and Culturally Diverse World* (Oxford University Press, forthcoming).